THE

CASE

FOR

BIG

GOVERNMENT

The Public Square Book Series/Princeton University Press

Ruth O'Brien, *Series Editor*

Uncouth Nation: Why Europe Dislikes America
by Andrei S. Markovits

The Politics of the Veil *by Joan Wallach Scott*

Hidden in Plain Sight:
The Tragedy of Children's Rights from Ben Franklin to Lionel Tate
by Barbara Bennett Woodhouse

The Case for Big Government
by Jeff Madrick

The Posthuman Dada Guide: tzara and lenin play chess
by Andrei Codrescu

With Thanks to the Donors of the Public Square
President William P. Kelly, the CUNY Graduate Center

JEFF
MADRICK

THE

CASE

FOR

BIG

GOVERNMENT

With a new preface by the author

PRINCETON UNIVERSITY PRESS

PRINCETON AND OXFORD

Published by Princeton University Press, 41 William Street,
Princeton, New Jersey 08540
In the United Kingdom: Princeton University Press, 6 Oxford Street,
Woodstock, Oxfordshire OX20 1TW
press.princeton.edu

Second printing, and first paperback printing,
with a new preface and foreword, 2010
Paperback ISBN: 978-0-691-14620-1

The Library of Congress has cataloged the cloth
edition of this book as follows
Madrick, Jeffrey G.
The case for big government / Jeff Madrick.
p. cm. — (The public square book series)
Includes bibliographical references and index.
ISBN 978-0-691-12331-8 (hardcover : alk. paper) 1. United States—
Politics and government. 2. Organizational effectiveness—United States.
3. United States—Economic policy—2001–ꞏ I. Title.
JK421.M328 2009
320.973—dc22
2008029706

British Library Cataloging-in-Publication Data is available

This book has been composed in Perpetua Typeface
Printed on acid-free paper. ∞
Printed in the United States of America

3   5   7   9   10   8   6   4   2

For Samantha,

Harrison

and, of course,

Kim

■ ■ ■ ■

ACKNOWLEDGMENTS

Without two talented and caring people, this book would not have happened. Based on lectures at the City University of New York, the book was enthusiastically and kindly initiated and supported by Ruth O'Brien of CUNY and my editor, Brigitta van Rheinberg of Princeton University Press, now its editor-in-chief. Their help was invaluable. Peter Dougherty, Princeton University Press Director, was a constant supporter of the book as well. Again, many thanks. Two researchers in particular, Jason Harle and Nikolaos Papanikolaou, provided material and insights well beyond what was demanded of them. They deserve more than casual mention. Thanks also to the highly competent editorial and publicity staff of Princeton for their enthusiasm and professionalism. And sincere thanks also to two anonymous reviewers, as well as Brigitta van Rheinberg, whose diligent and good-faith comments were critical to the final outcome of this book.

Personal thanks must also go to my wife, Kim Baker, for her many insights, careful reading, and persistent encouragement. I would also like to thank Edward M. Kennedy, the senior senator from Massachusetts, for a lesson learned when I worked with him. America is a work in progress. It is not a finished product.

CONTENTS

....

FOREWORD

....

Ruth O'Brien

Some books resonate. Some books profit from, and help instill, "a political time" to be heard. These same books, published in such a significant moment, wake us up—they jolt us with the realization that, had they been published a tad earlier, they might not have been well heard. They could have been passed over or ignored. Conceived in the depths of the second Bush administration, when the oracle on the rock was Wall Street high-risk speculative capitalism, Jeff Madrick's timely book *The Case for Big Government* offered us a different narrative about our present, our past, and our future that only now hits home.

Madrick's book is titled the case for *big* government. Although *The Case for Big Government* is authentic, or a "calling" as he describes it, the book is not about merely designing another New Deal, New Frontier, or Great Society. Nor is it limited to revealing an absence of reform—reform that the 2008 national elections showed us we lacked for over two generations. No, the book is both more subtle and ambitious, as Madrick's original wistful title—"The Purpose of Government"—indicated. This title encapsulated the simple, yet profound thesis that governments have purpose. Governments exist; they are built to do something. Through time governments have provided for their demos, their subjects, their citizens, their people, and their peoples. Representative democratic governments cannot be equated with umpires or worse—guarding the security of the shipyard for their own take or self-interest, ensuring that no one messes with the rough-and-tumble speculative capitalism of the twenty-first century despite all the public harm income inequality creates.

What, as Madrick so poignantly asks, *was* the purpose of past American governments? Why did the government get blamed when the nation lost its way in the late 1970s with the oil crisis and stagflation? How did the myth of laissez-faire capitalism get moored and become so firmly anchored? How could this myth help propagate income inequality, among other economic and social problems, and yet "the government" remain the problem?

Now published in paperback, *The Case for Big Government* is being heard. For many, the government is no longer the problem. For others, namely critics on Fox News and in other right-wing organizations, the very term "big government," they hope, will be heard again for their own rhetorical purposes— to defeat another Democratic administration. Clearly, the very idea of government has sparked a debate, but because we live in a different time, a historic time, a time in which capitalism as we knew it crashed, never to return—or at least not return in its former twenty-first-century incarnation without the holes being patched up, water-safe, with great reforms and initiatives. But then again, who knows what the future will hold? The Obama administration's reforms could be deep and structural, demarcating government's returned purpose. Or they could be leaky boards, nailed and bent to suit global capitalism's times. Health care, bank reform, more economic stimulus packages, tax reform, energy legislation—under the Obama administration each could push us in so many different directions. And no doubt, each direction takes us close to the rocky shore. It is in this way that Madrick's book introduces arguments that stimulated and will continue to stimulate worthy debate in the Public Square.

PREFACE TO THE PAPERBACK EDITION

·····················

America had been living a free-market myth for a generation until the credit crisis of 2008 and 2009 descended on the nation—and the world. One expression of that myth, found frequently on the editorial pages of the popular media, was that government does not grow economies, business does. In other words, government, don't meddle where you're not needed. Politicians are even easier to belittle than government itself.

I have spent much of my professional life making the opposite point. Government does indeed grow economies. It creates jobs and it produces prosperity. When politicians make correct decisions, they indeed make economies grow. There is no example of a major rich nation in the world whose government does not educate its children and teenagers; build its roads, bridges, superhighways, and airports; establish regulatory bodies to minimize financial busts; develop sanitation and water systems, and health care standards; support those who are temporarily unemployed; and provide a public pension to the elderly and a subsidy to the poor.

This is the call of big government. Label it proportional government if the words "big government" bother you. It is people getting together to do what they believe they must. And, yes, this is what good politicians do. Let's call it like it is.

As economies grow larger, societies more populous, scientific and social knowledge deeper, and interconnections more complex, government grows as well. At least in societies that succeed. Given the record of economic growth of today's rich nations over the past one hundred to two hundred years—some

200 or 300 times larger than when they started—big government's record is remarkably good. Politicians must have called some good shots.

If we analyze a little more deeply the place and purpose of government, we will find that when government works as it should, it is also typically the leading agent of change. As economies progress, societies learn more, and expectations rise, government's main purpose is to manage, foster, and adapt to this change. It is a profound task. The bipartisan attempts in the United States in recent years to resurrect a universal set of government rules and obligations based in the American past violates the history of the U.S. government, which adapted, often radically, to change. It looked ahead, not backward.

Fearing the future and aiming to protect established interests, influential forces invariably opposed new obligations for government. Some opposed financing the canals in the 1820s. Others did not want government to build free primary schools in the 1830s and 1840s, or the high schools in the late 1800s. Still others late in the early 1900s fought the development of government-built sanitation and water systems that made the cities possible. Some fought vaccination programs and health research.

As economies became industrial and manufacturing jobs spread, there were those who insisted unemployment was the fault of the worker him- or herself, not the business cycle or competition. There were those who were opposed to protecting labor rights concerning hours worked, job safety, and a minimum wage. Although financial boom and bust took their toll every twenty years since the 1790s, and almost bankrupted the nation in the very early 1900s, there were still those opposed to creating a central bank to mitigate disruption and regulate unstable financial markets.

All myths are by definition simplistic. The one which became entrenched in the late 1970s and early 1980s had as its core claim that government's presence was usually an impediment to prosperity and that the best course for the American economy was to reduce aggressively government's size and reach. So popular was this destructive notion that the end of the "era of big government" was announced proudly in 1996 by a Democratic president, Bill Clinton.

In the past thirty years, government, with a few exceptions, did not adequately sustain and nurture society, or help it adapt to change. Government invested less in America, it regulated less, and it led less. It was a lost generation.

The financial crisis occurred because of this widespread disdain for and distrust of government. Under ideological pressure to which both political parties subscribed and under the influence of powerful vested interests, government stepped back and gave financial markets largely free rein. Very risky investments were made with enormous levels of debt; the failure of one firm could take down the entire industry. Common sense was discarded and new, highfalutin theories about the rationality and efficiency of markets dominated thinking at the best universities, the halls of Congress, and the boardroom of the nation's central bank. Always, the argument was the financial community understood risk better than any government could.

As I mentioned, I have opposed these views for many years. When one combs the serious academic evidence about how and why economies grow, no case can be made that big government or even high taxes impede economic growth over time. History offers no lesson about the values of minimal government. There has never been a laissez-faire modern economy. To the contrary, the evidence shows that government typically contributed vitally to growth. As odd as it is to have to say this, without effective government, America would be poor today.

The lost faith in government has affected almost all aspects of life detrimentally in America in the last generation: health care, education, retirement security, the quality and durability of jobs, family time available to raise children, rising prison populations, and the nation's wealth itself. As I write this, financial instability and its consequences dominate tragically the lives of us all.

The major question today is whether the deep setbacks caused by the credit crisis will awaken the nation to the need to revitalize government again. If America returns to the norms of the past thirty years, the nation will not succeed. America stepped back from its obligations and responsibility many times in its history, but there is ample precedent to show how America can rise again to do what it must. A start is to recognize the true and extensive purpose of government. Government is not always good. It requires vigilance and weeding. But it also requires the confidence and understanding of its people. These it must earn, but the people in turn must also learn their own history, free of ideological cant and petty anger. This book is meant to present the argument for government, not in ideological terms, but quietly and based on the evidence.

PART I

····················

GOVERNMENT
AND CHANGE
IN AMERICA

The Danger of an Ideology

IT IS CONVENTIONAL wisdom in America today that high levels
of taxes and government spending diminish America's prosperity. The claim strikes a deep intuitive chord, not only among
those on the Right, but also among many on today's Left. It has
become so obvious to so many over the last thirty years, it
hardly seems to require demonstration any longer. It is apparently so widely accepted by the public and rolls off the tongues
of policymakers from both parties with such fluency that one
would think the evidence needn't even be gathered. Republican
followers of Ronald Reagan remain the most ardent support-
ers of the idea. "Closed case: tax cuts mean growth," wrote
former Tennessee Republican Senator Fred Thompson, who
can't seem to imagine there could be an alternative argument.[1]
Dick Armey, the former Texas congressman, has made almost
a career of criticizing those who argue otherwise. Armey, who
holds a doctorate in economics, claims to provide academic
proof for the case against taxes and government, and sarcasti-
cally accuses those who dare disagree of fearing "big thoughts."[2]
The leading Republican lobbying groups—notably the Club of
Growth, run by Stephen Moore who once worked for Armey

in Congress, and Americans for Freedom, headed by the conservative firebrand Grover Norquist—make lower taxes their principal cause. Deregulation and minimal government oversight of markets go hand in hand with this argument, other cornerstones of the Reagan revolution kept alive in subsequent decades.

Many of today's Democrats only partially disagree. To the conventional Democrat today, tax increases and increased government spending are by and large to be minimized and at best avoided. This is partly simple electoral calculation; holding any other position is considered politically destructive because the public has been so well convinced of its merit. But it has also become a matter of belief, as Democrats revise their traditional views and make deficit reduction their primary government objective. In fact, many Democrats had a hand in persuading the public of the dangers of big government. President Clinton successfully raised taxes on better-off Americans in 1993, but with the express purpose of reducing the federal deficit, not developing new social programs. The triumph of Republicans in the 1994 congressional elections reinforced the perception that American public opinion had turned against government. Clinton, determined to win a second term, abided by the sentiment. He proudly announced the new position of the centrist Democrats: "The era of big government is over," he said with some fanfare in his State of the Union address of January, 1996, the year of his presidential re-election bid. For all the success of the Clinton tax increase, the Democratic Leadership Council (DLC), which Clinton helped found in the mid-1980s, continued to urge Democrats in later years to tread lightly regarding tax increases and the new social programs that require them. An "American Dream Initiative" in 2006, put forward by the DLC, recommended paying for modest new proposals only by closing tax loopholes, and demanded that no new programs should be enacted without a way of financing them. By then, Democrats generally favored more tax cuts for the middle class, and by 2008 the leading Democratic presidential candidates only agreed to raise taxes on high-income Americans. Without more tax money—PAYGO, as it was called—there could be few social initiatives. The Republicans had won strategically. Some Democrats also emphatically put the best face on the economic status of workers over these years, claiming a degree of success that was exaggerated, in an effort to make a case for minimizing new government social programs and to justify their political strategy.[3]

Federal deregulation also reflects such attitudes about government. The lax federal oversight under George W. Bush has taken an increasingly obvious toll, most notably in the credit crisis of 2008 with hundreds of billions of dollars of losses accrued at major financial institutions, but also in areas such as food and drug safety, airline traffic and safety, and most tragically with the aftermath of Hurricane Katrina. But few Democrats acknowledged how much they themselves contributed to a weakened regulatory attitude in the United States. Deregulation began to gain influence with the Nixon Administration in the early 1970s, but Jimmy Carter was a sincere believer and, aside from airline and trucking deregulation, which were arguably sensible, gave financial deregulation a decided push. Under Clinton, much of the New Deal regulatory apparatus designed to restrain financial market excesses was formally and proudly eliminated in 1999, though de facto erosions of the famed Glass-Steagall restriction were underway for a decade.

When Clinton had hundreds of billions of dollars of budget surpluses to bestow in the late 1990s, he left federal spending on transportation, education, and poverty programs below the spending levels reached as a proportion of national income (the Gross Domestic Product) under his Republican predecessor, George H. W. Bush, or under President Reagan. To meet his social goals, Clinton generally resorted to tax credits, despite the reduction in growth of military spending made possible by the end of the Cold War, to provide help for the working poor and the adoption of tax-advantaged programs to expand health insurance, retirement savings, and the affordability of college education.

Such an approach fit neatly into the new conventional wisdom that bigger government was a danger to prosperity. It also fit the ascending ideology of greater reliance on free markets. A tax break may encourage savings by exempting investment from income tax until retirement or raising incentives to work by creating a tax credit even as one's income rises. But the market does the rest of the work, not government. The same faith in markets of course motivated broad deregulation. "Market incentives" became the new buzz phrase among middle-of-the road Democratic economists. Such an approach also had the great virtue of not requiring a tax increase to support a social program. But in fact it was costly to government; tax revenues were lost. Meanwhile, with Clinton's encouragement, Wall Street hadn't had such a friendly response from Democrats in anyone's memory.

Some reforming of social programs was certainly necessary. Using subsidies rather than outright handouts can often make sense. Markets do have efficient distributive capacities which should be utilized as often as is sensible. But the new focus did not represent the return of clear-eyed pragmatism that it promised. Quite the opposite, it was an ideological turning point that moved the nation to the adoption of an antigovernment faith. "We know government doesn't have all the answers," Clinton said in his 1996 State of the Union address. But, though some progressive programs had indeed been overly ambitious and failed, no one ever promised that government did have all the answers. By citing this straw man, Clinton had joined those who painted the government with an ideological broad brush of disapproval, and he brought the Democratic Party with him.

Nobelist economist Milton Friedman, famed mentor and revered hero to Armey and others, was before his death in 2006 the leading and most articulate academic economist in favor of this antigovernment position. Friedman's influence over theorists and policymakers alike was serious, and his rise to prominence simply remarkable. In the 1950s and 1960s, he was widely considered an extremist, if a well-schooled, intelligent, and articulate one. The frigid reception to his classic free-market book of 1962, *Capitalism and Freedom,* reflected the progressive attitudes of the Kennedy-Johnson years. But he pulled the entire mainstream profession unexpectedly in his direction in later years. By the 1970s, the book had become a best-seller, and his apostasy had become gospel to many.

Looking back, Friedman wrote in the preface to a 2002 edition of *Capitalism and Freedom* that people's experience with government expansion since 1962 had convinced them his economic philosophy was right.[4] In fact, the conservative movement's great friend was not the book's insights, which were simplistic, but the damaging hyperinflation of the 1970s, which Friedman and others misleadingly attributed to government spending directly. By the late 1970s, most of America was convinced that government was the issue. It was effective simple politics and bad analysis. In Reagan's 1980 debate with Jimmy Carter before the November presidential election, he told Americans they had to live with inflation, not because they lived too well but because government did. The well-said message stuck in the mind of the public. After the debate, Reagan's approval ratings rose markedly in public opinion surveys, and he won easily a week later.[5]

Friedman offered much ideology but little evidence that big government was the root of the problem. The causes of inflation in the 1970s were far more complex than the growing money supply—the factor that Friedman emphasized and linked to growing federal spending.[6] Rising government budget deficits can contribute to inflation, but other equally or more prominent causes in this complex decade included the eightfold hike in oil prices by the cartel of exporting nations, remarkably bad crop supplies worldwide, a sudden downshift in productivity growth not anticipated by any economist, including Friedman, and the fall in the value of the dollar. As for the size of government, federal expenditures were only one percentage point higher in the first half of the 1970s as a proportion of GDP than they were in the first half of the 1960s, yet annual inflation started to rise rapidly in the early 1970s while annual consumer price inflation was only slightly more than 1 percent in the early 1960s. What of the budget deficits that horrified Americans in the 1970s? Even in the worst years of the 1970s, as a proportion of the economy budget deficits were not larger than they were during the worst years of George W. Bush's administration in the early 2000s, when inflation was mild.

But Friedman's argument about the dangers of government was politically effective for a variety of reasons, including weariness over the Vietnam War, the Watergate scandal, the counterculture, and national desegregation policies. It also found reinforcing echoes in America's nostalgia for an artificial laissez-faire past. Reagan was Friedman's translator. And the mythology remains with the nation. In his early campaigning for the Republican presidential campaign in 2008, Mike Huckabee, governor of Arkansas, and admirer of Reagan, put the old American myth simply. "The greatness of this country has never been in its government," he said in a speech before the

New Hampshire primary. "Any time the government gives something to us, they first have to take something from us."[7]

This book is a refutation of such assertions. The popular economic case against big government, including the more moderate Democratic version, does not stand up to the evidence. Big-government and high-tax nations do not grow systematically more slowly than nations with lower government spending as a proportion of the economy and lower tax rates. More precisely, big-government and high-tax nations elsewhere simply do not in the real world automatically undermine the capacity to produce more for an extra hour of work—its productivity. Peter Lindert of the University of California at Davis spent years compiling data on the subject in a 2004 book. There is, he concludes, a dramatic "conflict between intuition and evidence. It is well-known that higher taxes and transfers reduce productivity. Well-known—but unsupported by statistics and history."[8]

I am not arguing here that there is evidence that big government and high taxes are always and everywhere good. If government is managed poorly, it can have damaging effects. Can taxes be raised too high in the short run? Yes. High taxes can undermine motivation and incentives to work and invest, but economists who devotedly maintain that government undermines growth almost always seriously exaggerate these disincentives. Can social programs be poorly managed or counter productive? Yes.

What I am arguing is that judging by the careful assessment of economic achievements by nations with high taxes and large governments, and judging by American history itself, active and sizable government has been essential to growth and prosperity among the world's rich nations, including America. Any impact on incentives and any displacement of private spending by higher taxes have been well more than compensated for, history shows, by spending programs and regulatory functions that enhance growth. If tax revenues are used to invest productively in the nation's human capital, its infrastructure, its legal system, and the fair distribution of economic rewards, they have typically been essential to growth. These programs create the tools and assets that enable the private markets to function.

The book goes one step further. It argues that big or small government is not the critical criterion in economics. To the contrary, government's management of change is what is critical. And government is a key and arguably the main agent of change. Without an active government, a nation cannot respond adequately to its times. If it does not respond to new conditions, both economic growth and the ability to retain a nation's values will suffer. In the laboratory of the real world, the governments of rich nations have on balance been central to economic growth, and in the process have retained their citizens' faith in their nations' promise and social values. Does this mean government must be big? The lesson is that pragmatic government should prevail over any categorical or typically ideological dismissal of the uses of government, including Bill Clinton's. If what we think of as big government is necessary to manage change, and in a complex society it may well be, then we should pursue it actively and positively, and make it function well.

Today, an ideological antagonism toward government in the United States has deeply undermined the nation's capacity to deal with its rapidly changing times. These changes include rising competition around the globe, a marked worsening in wage growth and widening of income distribution since the 1970s, the rapidly rising costs of health care, an aging population, and the need for ever-more years of education. The two-worker family has become the nation's norm. The possibilities for advanced transportation and better energy use due to technological innovation have excitingly expanded, as transportation and other infrastructures, including public water systems, are allowed to decay. Change also includes constantly evolving ideas in America about who should participate in the full rights and opportunities of the nation, an evolution in American society that at first excluded and then progressively welcomed to the fold all manner of immigrants—from the early Germans and Swedes to the Irish, Italians, and Jews and ultimately Latinos. Over time, women, African Americans, Native Americans, and gays were also welcomed. Our knowledge about what is required to lead a full life changes as well. We now know, for example, how important early education is to human development. We are much more aware of the most subtle abuses of race and gender. And we believe that old age can be productive.

But today's conventional wisdom reflects a narrow view of government. Government, as Garry Wills notes, is thought to be a "necessary evil," a last resort.[9] In terms of the economy, the argument against government goes something like this. First, higher taxes will undermine the incentives of those who work and invest. Second, social programs are administered so poorly that they are a waste of resources, and moreover create dependencies among those who receive help. Finally, social spending crowds out the vibrant private sector, especially if it must be financed in the bond markets, and thereby undermines productivity. Regarding the nation's social and political values, the central complaint of advocates of less government—an age-old one among political conservatives—is that any intrusion of government reduces individual choice and freedom itself. Hence, for example, Friedman's book title, *Capitalism and Freedom*.

The empirical problem with the economic claims is that the economies of nations with high taxes and big governments have grown rapidly, are highly productive, and provide their citizens with a standard of living every bit the equivalent of America's and some argue superior to it. The problem with the political claims is that so-called big government has enlarged freedom by protecting civil rights, minimizing discrimination, giving people decent health care and the educational and economic tools to fulfill their lives, which ultimately contribute to further prosperity, and have withstood the return of totalitarianism everywhere in the West.[10] Democracy has simply thrived in "the welfare states" of Europe.

In fact, there really is no example of small government among rich nations. The size of government grew across all the world's rich nations, particularly in the twentieth century, and the rate of economic growth only increased. While Milton Friedman complained about the growth of government in the 1950s and the 1960s, the American economy never grew faster in its history, and the incomes of all Americans, discounted for inflation, doubled over less than twenty-five years—that is, grew by 100 percent. After the Reagan revolution of reduced taxes and deregulation, rapid growth in the standard of living was never recaptured except for a few years in the late 1990s. Since the 1970s, the income of a typical male has actually fallen, discounted for inflation, and typical family income grew by only 25 percent over more than thirty-five years, largely because spouses went to work.[11] People met the rest of their needs by borrowing heavily.

It is simply not the size of government spending or the level of taxes, but the composition and quality of the spending that affects how fast economies grow and standards of living improve. We are not discussing short-term economic policies here, but rather the long-term support of growth. Cuts in taxes will often temporarily help stimulate growth, but the latter is largely a liberal argument, derived from the philosophy first developed in the 1930s by the British economist John Maynard Keynes. The same (and even more potent) stimulatory effects can be temporarily attained by more government spending as well. The conservative argument for tax cuts is based on the dubious claim that such tax cuts result in more than merely modest incentives to work harder and invest more. It is not that big government is to be encouraged in and of itself. What we know is that nations with bigger governments have not as a rule grown more slowly than those with relatively smaller governments; to the contrary, they have sometimes grown faster. That can only be the case because their spending programs on balance enhance rather than detract from growth, fill the many gaps that markets cannot, and that regulations on balance make markets work better and minimize abuse and corruption. This rather easily demonstrable fact is but a heresy in modern America.

But government must change with the times to fulfill its central functions. A critical purpose of government, as noted, is to respond to and facilitate changing conditions in society and the economy in order to retain a nation's prosperity and its values. When business operates well, it also must and does respond to changing needs and wants. For government, one of the crucial benefits of democracy itself is that it creates ways to communicate new needs and takes note of shifting opinion and evolving knowledge. Democracy is thus critical to adapting to change. Free speech and open public discourse are components of democracy and thus essential to change. [12]

Social and economic conditions have changed rapidly and continually since the colonial years, and change today is not more profound than it has been in the past. But it is profound, nevertheless. The problem for government, as for many other institutions, is to reorient itself from proven successes in the past. Few talk about government as an agent of change.

Much of this book will be about how government has adapted to change in the past, and about identifying the ideological restraints that have kept the nation from adapting in recent decades. The implementation of experimental, pragmatic, and courageous policies, based on new conditions and pressing contemporary problems, was more common in America's history than is widely realized. Many want to believe otherwise— that a certain set of duties and obligations is more or less written in a foundation of stone. In today's America, radically new economic and social conditions have been ignored and neglected because of the high level of antagonism toward government and the resulting tendency to resort to historical narratives, based more on ideology than facts, to limit further uses of government. America has often—but not always—adapted to its needs.

The Evidence

The fastest growth of social programs in history—the rise of the so-called welfare state—took place in the rich Western nations and Japan over the three decades after 1950.[13] Yet, over that same period, the incomes of a typical family—indeed, of most families—grew at unprecedentedly rapid rates in all these nations, a period which even included the sharp rise in oil prices in the 1970s. No government of a Western nation today spends less than 10 percent of Gross Domestic Product (GDP) on its poor, unhealthy, or aged, for example—what are usually called social transfers— yet all are immensely wealthy by historical standards.[14] In addition to social transfers, they all spend significantly on education and infrastructure, and they all remain vibrant democracies as well.

Nevertheless, the case that big government is damaging is presented as open and shut. If so, the evidence supporting it should be as close to unambiguous as such economic evidence can possibly be. Yet a reading of the literature shows that, for all its alleged obviousness, the advocates have not remotely proved the point. To the contrary, no case can be reasonably made that government has systematically impeded growth.

Martin Feldstein, Harvard economist, president of the National Bureau of Economic Research, and head of the Council of Economic Advisers under President Reagan, is one of the leading figures in the post-Friedman generation of economists who persistently cites the damage done by big government. Feldstein believes high taxes invariably suppress incentives to work and invest; social programs, if occasionally necessary, are too costly, inefficient, and usually undermine individual effort; and government spending displaces private enterprise, thereby reducing the economy's productivity. Feldstein often focuses on the issue of high taxes.

"Economists recognized," Feldstein wrote in 1994, referring to the 1980s, "that it was through improved incentives rather than through increased demand that a sustained increase in national income could be achieved. Research studies emphasized the adverse effects of high marginal tax rates and of the rules governing transfer programs like unemployment insurance and Social Security that penalized work and saving."[15]

This is a vast overgeneralization. By no means did all economists agree with this proposition, but it was a fairly conventional anti-Keynesian argument made by a growing school of conservative economists. They claimed that tax cuts do not stimulate the economy by increasing purchasing power, as Keynes argued but, as noted, by increasing incentives to work and invest. The latter means that permanently lower taxes should produce a more vibrant economy. While respected studies were undertaken that supported Feldstein's claims, others completely refuted the assessment even in the 1980s.

Feldstein got a chance to put one of his sweeping claims to the test under Bill Clinton. He argued that the Clinton tax increase of three percentage points on high-income Americans, implemented in 1993, would clearly demonstrate the anti-growth impact of higher taxes. The reduced incentives to work due to the tax bite taken out of income would be seen in lower reported incomes by these individuals. Incomes were indeed lower in 1993, as Feldstein reported—and knew about at the time he finished the research, which gave him confidence to make the case.

The reason those incomes were lower, however, was well-documented later: wealthier individuals were able to move their income into 1992 tax returns, at the time the legislation was passed but before it went into effect. The lower incomes of 1993 were thus not related to reduced incentives to work and invest, but to clever strategies to report income in 1992 that would have normally been reported in 1993. In fact, in 1994, despite the higher tax rates, reported incomes for well-off individuals rose rapidly on average in 1994 and afterwards, the opposite of Feldstein's prediction. The high-income individuals kept working hard, taking more risk, and making a lot more money, even though the higher income tax rates remained. Moderately higher taxes simply did not undermine incentives to work, a serious failure of the Feldstein hypothesis.[16]

Another major claim of economists antagonistic to government programs is that social spending for programs like unemployment insurance, Social Security, and Medicare will as noted either undermine incentives to work and save or so displace private investment and business spending that they will reduce the efficiency and potential growth of the American economy. In other words, social transfers—usually including tax financed spending for housing, unemployment, pensions, health care and welfare for the poor—will reduce the economy's productivity or output per hour of work. People will work less hard, the taxes themselves distort markets and make the economy less efficient, and government spending is largely a waste that displaces more productive private spending. Harvard's Robert Barro is among the leaders of this group, which typically tries to compares growth rates among different countries.[17]

Such studies must show a clear relationship between slower growth, lower GDP per capita, or reduced productivity to higher levels of government spending or higher taxes. But when studies done by Barro and others that purport to show government's deleterious effect on growth or levels of income are probed by other experts, they do not hold up. Joel Slemrod, an economist at the University of Michigan, did a comprehensive and respected review of the studies in a classic paper, and says that the conclusion that big government undermines growth does not pass closer inspection. Economists Sergio Rebelo of Northwestern and William Easterly of New York University, neither of whom would describe himself as politically liberal, also conclude the statistical relationships found are "fragile." In other words, slightly different assumptions or sets of data undermine the conclusions. Given how strenuously antigovernment researchers make their case, why is it impossible for them to prove it unambiguously?[18]

Peter Lindert, who is a mainstream economist, has done broad comparative analyses of experiences in Europe and North America and concludes unreservedly that "the net national costs of social transfers and of the taxes that finance them, are essentially zero. They do not bring the GDP the costs that much of the Anglo-American literature have imagined." Lindert goes on: "Whether one looks at the level or rates of change, one can find no clear negative relationship between social spending and GDP per capita. . . . Neither simple raw correlations nor the careful weighing of the apparent sources of growth shows any negative net effect of all that redistribution."[19]

Who is the lay reader to believe? The case does not rest on simply choosing selectively the research studies that support the view. The ultimate point is that, if the case made that big government is detrimental to economic growth is as simple and unambiguous as some economists and political commentators claim it is, not to mention politicians, the statistical evidence should be easy to demonstrate and virtually impossible to refute. The opposite is true, as we've seen. The studies supporting the case generally fall apart on closer analysis.

What is going on? Some economists make truly simplistic analyses, ignoring such basic factors as the business cycle. For example, as Lindert notes, some will claim that that economies grow faster when social spending falls as a proportion of GDP. But the measured fall in social spending as a proportion of GDP is a function of the rising GDP during economic expansion, so it does not demonstrate any causal relationship.[20]

There are more subtle analyses and distorting assumptions, however. Lindert says that some of the most respected researchers often "torture" the data, redoing their computer programs with different data and assumptions until they find the conclusions they seek. Others do simulations of real-world conditions that are not "real world" at all. In demonstrating the antigovernment claims, some economists simply presume that all government spending basically goes down a black hole and has no economic value whatsoever. Others, somewhat more honest, will at least treat the tax revenues neutrally. But few deal with the facts as they really are, which shows that many of these spending programs have positive value.

As a result, the conclusions of many of these studies defy common sense. Many claim to demonstrate, for example, that a higher income tax so undermines the private economy that it necessarily results in a loss of GDP greater than the tax itself. Based on several of these studies done by reputable economists, for example, Sweden's GDP is now 10 to 50 percent lower than it otherwise would have been. Thus, if Sweden had only cut its taxes to the U.S. level and similarly limited its welfare state, it could be so much wealthier today that it would possibly be the richest nation in the world by far.[21] France's consumption would be 20 percent greater than it is today if it only adopted U.S. tax rates, according to one study.[22] What can they be waiting for, one wonders?

Because in fact these high-tax economies actually do well, it follows that what happens in the real world is that much of that tax money is spent constructively, on programs that inspire a sense of confidence, improve productivity, and promote good health and education. Even when there are moderate disincentives to invest and work, many of the programs are oriented to minimize these. For example, even high levels of unemployment insurance, a particular bête noir of conservatives, can remove less productive workers from the labor force and minimize any damaging consequences from shirking work. Regulations, in turn, enable markets to work better by making information more available and reducing abuse and corruption. Such regulation can save money, even if costly to comply with.

Let's return to the case of Sweden. Many critics argued that its welfare state had gone too far by the 1980s—taxes were too high, and wages too generous. Incomes compared to the rest of the wealthy countries were no longer near the top of the tables. Market-oriented adjustments were made in Sweden, including tax cuts, and conditions improved. But Sweden did not cut taxes or social spending nearly to the U.S. levels, or even to Britain's. To the contrary, social transfers remained a very high proportion of national income, roughly 30 percent of GDP, not including education expenditures. The United States expends about 13 percent of GDP on such social transfers (Social Security, Medicare, unemployment insurance, housing, and poverty).

Yet, with such high levels of social transfers, the growth rate of GDP per person since the mid-1990s in Sweden was as high through the mid-2000s as the growth rate of the United States or almost any European nation—many of which equaled America's GDP growth rate per capita during this period (which included the Clinton boom years).[23] Sweden's average compensation per hour paid to its manufacturing workers is about equal to America's. (To make the wages comparable in this comparison, they are adjusted for what is called purchasing power parity—what goods and services the wage actually buys.) Sweden's productivity, which is according to many economists inevitably damaged by high levels of social transfers, has not fallen ignominiously. It is about 88 percent of America's level (see table 1).

The experience of other rich nations is even more telling. Let's keep in mind that Germany, France, and Italy spend almost as much on social transfers as does Sweden in terms of GDP, and the other Nordic nations spend roughly the same amount. This means that citizens enjoy free or very inexpensive, education, health care, and usually child care. The quality of health care and education through high school is very high. Time off for working mothers with children is shockingly generous from an American perspective. Thus, the typical citizen receives a great deal even before he or she earns a wage.

Yet, on top of that, and even despite such spending, German businesses pay its manufacturing workers 127 percent of

TABLE 1
Comparing Productivity and Wages in Other Nations (2004 dollars)

Country	Productivity	Manufacturing compensation (using purchasing power parity)
USA	100	100
Sweden	88	98
Germany	92	127
France	107	91
Netherlands	100	101
Norway	125	110

Source: Mishel et al., *The State of Working America 2006/2007*, p. 329 and p. 342

American levels and Norway 110 percent. Despite the generous social programs, manufacturing workers in about half of the two dozen wealthiest nations earn as much than their counterparts in the United States. Productivity is higher in France, the Netherlands, and Norway than in the United States, and comparable in several other nations.

America's GDP per person is the highest in the world (with the special exception of Belgium). The main reason is that a very high proportion of both men and women work, and Americans on average work more hours than do their counterparts in other rich nations.[24] Thus, America does provide more jobs than most other nations. This is not a small achievement.[25] But it is probably largely because it pays lower wages, especially near the bottom of the spectrum. Jobs for those in the prime working ages in Europe are plentiful. About the same proportion of people between the ages of twenty-five and fifty-four work in Europe as in America. In Sweden, a higher proportion of women work than in the United States, partly because of family friendly laws for working mothers. Labor participation is especially high in the United States among young workers.[26]

In sum, America's productivity is 15 percent higher than the average of nations in the Organization for Economic and Co-operative Development (OECD), the two dozen or so richest nations in the world. But it is lower than a half dozen nations with much higher taxes and rates of social spending. And roughly half of the OECD countries pay higher or equal wages to workers in manufacturing, and almost all provide substantially more benefits than does the United States, including mostly free education and health care.[27]

■ ■ ■ ■ ■

Let us now look at how the changing size of American government may or may not have affected U.S. prosperity in recent years. Friedman's 2002 criticism of big government followed hard on the heels of the Clinton boom of the late 1990s, when the nation's productivity rose rapidly for the first time since the early 1970s. One would have thought, given Friedman's claims about the nation's disappointment with big government and his warnings about high taxes, that the proportion of national income collected as federal taxes fell sharply during the Clinton boom. In the years preceding the boom, however, tax receipts rose above their earlier levels and during the boom itself reached 20 percent of GDP, much higher than at any other time since the final years of World War II. Even federal spending—though it grew more slowly under Clinton, largely because of the peace dividend following the Cold War and less rapid increases in health care costs—had fallen as a proportion of income only to the levels of the early 1970s. At that level of spending in the 1970s, inflation was beginning to rise rapidly; not so, in the Clinton years. The causal relationship is far from simple. Indeed, there often is no relationship.

Some still argue that the 1981 income tax cuts under Reagan produced the Clinton boom. Given that they occurred fifteen years earlier, the claim is far-fetched on the face of it. Many also conveniently neglect the argument they would have made had there been a Democrat in office, which is that under Reagan federal spending increased rapidly. Military spending increased by roughly a full percentage point of GDP, Medicare spending rose rapidly, and interest on the soaring budget deficits rose by well more than one percentage point of GDP. If their contentions were consistent, growth would have been undermined by such spending. Price Fishback, a mainstream economist and historian, who is not left of center, writes: "In fact, Reagan and George H.W. Bush looked more like Keynesians than any of the peacetime presidents."[28]

Furthermore, Reagan did not reduce the nation's tax burden, he shifted it. While income tax rates were cut, payroll taxes to pay for Social Security and Medicare were markedly increased. Total taxes as a proportion of GDP were about the same in Reagan's last year in office as they were in three out of four of Jimmy Carter's years as president.[29]

Despite the lower income tax rates as well as reductions in regulations and lax implementation of those that remained on the books, productivity adjusted for the ups and downs of the business cycle did not improve under Reagan or his successor, George H.W. Bush. According to the ascending free-market ideology, these should have improved incentives. The productivity take-off began in 1996, not long after the Clinton income tax increase. Feldstein, Armey and others predicted that tax increase would have the opposite effect.

■ ■ ■ ■ ■

Friedman's ideal world, one deduces, was the economy he imagined reigned in the nineteenth century, when government spending and control over the economy was least, or so the advocates of this view claim. There may have been financial panics, big busts, deep recessions, and corruption in the 1800s, but the nation, on balance, flourished, goes the argument. Workers may have been poor by modern standards, but average wages discounted for inflation rose inexorably if cyclically over time and poverty was reduced. Gross Domestic Product per capita—the nation's income per man, woman, and child—rose severalfold discounted for inflation over the century, always making up for recessionary dips within a few years and then rising higher. By 1900, and probably earlier, America was the richest nation in the world, and also the most productive—generating more goods and services per hour of work than any other nation.[30]

In the twentieth century, there were complications, according to the argument. Government began to spend more as a proportion of GDP, a progressive income tax was introduced and made permanent, and a broad set of regulations was adopted, first at the turn of the century and then more vigorously with the New Deal of the 1930s, the Great Society of the 1960s, and the Nixon presidency of the early 1970s. The Progressives believed they were helping shield many from the harsh pains of volatile markets and the unfair balance of power in favor of business. But in making life more "fair," they both undermined the economy and individual motivation, according to Friedman and like-minded thinkers who by and large minimized the personal pain suffered in the twentieth-century economy.

The key problem with the Friedman argument is that in the first three quarters of the century, despite higher taxes and the Great Depression of the 1930s, America prospered as never before, and Americans worked very hard as well despite growing social transfers. An agricultural economy in the early 1800s cannot fairly be compared to an industrial economy in the 1900s. But by the second half of the nineteenth century, America was fast becoming an industrial economy, based on heavy industry. In this period, the great oil, steel, and aluminum companies were born; the railroads were built; mass-produced consumer products like cigarettes and breakfast cereals spread; and the national retail chains were established. The cities also began to grow. And the economy grew rapidly, while government revenues were around 6 or 7 percent of GDP.

But the economy on average grew no faster in those years—which saw deep recessions and countless strained and often ruined lives—than in the later years of the twentieth century, and in particular in the twenty-five years after World War II, when federal, state, and local government spending eventually reached roughly 30 percent of GDP and income levels in America became more equal.

U.S. history in the 1900s provides a working model for examining the potential deleterious effects of higher taxes in particular. Nancy L. Stokey, of the University of Chicago, and Sergio Rebelo of Northwestern, did a careful statistical analysis of the rate of growth over this period as American tax rates increased. The income tax was established in 1913, at which time taxes came to 2 percent of GDP in 1913. It rose to 15 percent in 1942. The economists adjusted for the business cycle, including the Great Depression. According to the conventional wisdom, there should be evidence of a reduced rate of economic growth on average as tax rates rose. But there is none. The authors conclude that, "this large rise in income tax rates produced no noticeable effect on the average growth rate of the economy."

Friedman's own claims in *Capitalism and Freedom* initially seemed odd because he made them against this background of a robust economy in the 1950s and 1960s, America's "golden age" of growth. *Capitalism and Freedom* was a book of popular essays about the superiority of the free market, including the distribution of most social goods like pensions, education, and health care, and the great dangers to prosperity of social spending. But it was based largely on speeches made in 1956, and much of his analysis and writing was presumably done earlier—perhaps too early to realize how well the economy was actually doing. At the point of his writing, a postwar recession in the late 1940s was still fresh in memory, and there was another recession in 1953 and 1954. Yet all along, even with the economic downturns, the economy was on balance growing rapidly over the 1950s and 1960s, as were worker incomes.

Friedman's central claim that growing government undermined personal political and civil freedom was not borne out. His later followers, like Dick Armey, always couch the argument for low taxes as a patriotic defense of individual freedom. The grassroots organization Armey formed and headed after leaving government is indeed called FreedomWorks, and has as its motto, "Lower Taxes, Less Government, More Freedom."

Yet all the welfare states that Friedman warned about remain sound, vibrant democracies, and some new ones were added to the list, such as Spain and Portugal. Spain spends 19 percent of GDP on welfare, including unemployment, health care, pensions, housing, and poverty, while Portugal spends more than 15 percent—all more than the United States spends at 13 percent of GDP.[31] The failure of Soviet central planning was helpful to Friedman's cause, but it did not serve as a useful example for the argument he was making. The Soviet Union started as a totalitarian state; it did not evolve into one because government began to intrude in free markets. More recently, the experiment with free markets in Russia did not prevent a return of authoritarianism.

And was freedom undermined in America during the period Friedman explores? Historical strides were made in civil rights and women's rights at this time; the elderly were raised out of poverty en masse. In the 1950s, nearly one in three over sixty-five was poor; by the 1970s, only one in ten was poor. The poverty rate for all Americans was cut by at least ten percentage points from around 22 percent to 11 or 12 percent. Americans attended college in growing proportion. Nearly two thirds would own their own homes. All these added to freedom on balance, by all but the most narrow definition. Setbacks there were, and sacrifices as well. Busing to integrate schools affected working-class people more than others, to take a bitter example. But in spite of Friedman's dire warnings, large steps were taken to promote the equality the nation promised.

Looking-Back Narratives from the Right and Left

The romantic view of the limited role of government in America's economic history in the 1800s is simply wrong. Despite a national distrust of central government, Washington exercised its power often and sometimes well. Laissez-faire—hands off, basically—remained the nation's sensibility, but the philosophy was violated in practice time and again. National government frequently had a strong and defining influence, even when its expenditures were a small share of total income. Government policies, when they were most effective, were experimental and often bold, changed pragmatically with the times, and were not beholden to an ideology even in the time of Adam Smith's great popularity under Jefferson.

In early America, the national government protected civil and property rights, set rules, did indeed have a tax policy of substantial tariffs, and had serious control over the nation's economy through its often radical land policies. Its courts established a competition policy. It invested in transportation, education, and health care. Such public investment was critical to growth. Federal, state, and local governments often organized their social programs well, minimizing deleterious impacts on personal motivation and waste. And programs whose primary objectives are to make society more equitable and decent can foster growth by enhancing optimism, a sense of fairness, and reducing discrimination in markets, particularly for labor (which is always detrimental to growth). Such programs may help get the most out of human resources by assuring that for all that hard work, abiding by the law, and taking risk will be fairly and reasonably rewarded.

This is not to say that government always spent its money well or efficiently. There were errors and the dangers of bureaucratic inefficiency were sometimes evident. Commentators look back to find in the nation's history what they want to find. Dependence on such "looking-back narratives" typically reflects rising confusion and uncertainty. Commentators call upon history and the reputation of great men for authority. Some of America's early patriarchs were great men, but the phrase, "Founding Fathers," itself reflects a peculiar dependency on a special wisdom that simply defies human boundaries. It is reminiscent of the attachment the ancient Greeks had to their many gods, with the exception that unlike the well-known flaws of the Greek pantheon America does not easily accept the flaws of their early heroes. The Constitution was a brilliant result of the talents of the Founding Fathers and a document for a new age, but it was surely not "sacred," as Dick Armey likes to call it.[32] Books about the true brilliance of the Founding Fathers were especially popular amid the confusion and search for answers of the early 2000s, and a favorite pastime was to determine what the Founding Fathers truly thought and did in the early years of the nation—and what they would have thought and done today. One such book is called *What Would the Founders Do? Our Questions, Their Answers,* written by an editor of *The National Review.*[33] These books, if well-intentioned and sometimes intelligent, were more a reflection of a nation looking to rid itself of confusion as painlessly as possible, and the books had a decidedly conservative cast, mostly restoring the federalists to a place equal to or superior to Jefferson's.

The U.S. Constitution, barely adopted at the Constitutional Convention in 1787, is similarly invoked often as inviolable authority. The faith placed in it also has a disturbing quality in a modern nation. The Right and in some measure the Left read an authority into the Constitution to support their present-day views that can't truly be warranted. Progressive taxes were never conceived of by the Founding Fathers or written into the Constitution, says one conservative activist, who has made a career of opposing income taxes.[34] Of course, the Sixteenth Amendment made such taxes constitutional, but this was allegedly a usurpation of an earlier and surer wisdom. If the Founding Fathers were against it, the argument of semi-divine faith goes, so should we be.

The Constitution and the Bill of Rights are cut many ways. They are called upon to support those favoring a right to choice for women and those unalterably opposed to it. The legality of gun control is to be determined by uncovering the Constitution's true meaning, again supplying arguments to both sides. The right, or not, to free speech similarly draws contrasting support from the Constitution—and on and on. The rise of "originalism" (as distinguished from "original intent")— what the legislators really meant by the new laws when they were passed—is another "looking back" narrative. The argument is hardly unsophisticated, but there is no escaping its ideological uses. We must abide by this original two-hundred-year-old context, states originalism, famously advocated by Supreme Court Judge Antonin Scalia, as if the Framers ever truly agreed on this themselves.[35]

There are a variety of scholarly arguments to refute this misleading claim, not least that the Framers themselves wanted the Constitution to be flexible and readily applied to new circumstances (as did legislators of the laws they made). Justice Stephen Breyer offers a penetrating counterargument about the Constitution's flexibility.[36] The establishment of a republic of checks and balances, The Bill of Rights, was a remarkable achievement. But the informal search for authority in the Constitution for so many contemporary issues is a sign of a nation astray and a nation afraid of the future.

What is the nation looking for in its past? In economics and social policy, the Right calls upon the alleged laissez-faire successes of the 1800s as a guide to the future. Personal freedom is central to their claims, and high taxes, social policies, and regulation are a threat to that freedom. Their view of personal freedom is a "negative" one, as the political philosopher Isaiah Berlin defined it. Government's intrusions on the individual's ability to, say, buy a house, choose a career, or save for retirement, in fact, should be limited.[37] In this view, Social Security is seen as an involuntary requirement to place one's retirement money aside—a violation of rights. Government health care deprives us of our choice of doctors and procedures. Freedom and individual responsibility require us to accept poverty as the plight of the untalented or lazy, rather than ameliorate it through government giveaways, which may require the poor to act in a certain way and deprive the better-off of choice by confiscating their income through taxes. The Right looks back to early America to justify this view.

Friedman puts it this way in *Capitalism and Freedom*:

Political freedom means the absence of coercion of a man by his fellow men. The fundamental threat to freedom is power to coerce, be it in the hands of a monarch, a dictator, an oligarchy, or a momentary majority. The preservation of freedom requires the elimination of such concentration of power to the fullest possible extent and the dispersal and distribution of whatever power cannot be eliminated—a system of checks and balances. By removing the organization of economic activity from the control of political authority, the market eliminates this source of coercive power. It enables economic strength to be a check to political power rather than a reinforcement.[38]

The Left's view of freedom is traditionally close to Berlin's "positive" category. Not long after Friedman wrote the above, Lyndon Johnson put it this way in a 1968 speech: "The man who is hungry, who cannot find work or educate his children, who is bowed by want, that man is not fully free."[39] Roosevelt announced his own set of economic rights in his 1944 State of the Union address, but they went too far for the American public or Congress to accept. They included a right to a decent job, a good education, and adequate, modern health care.[40]

The protection of freedom has been a highly malleable concept in American history. All favor freedom, but its interpretation varies with the person and with the times. As the historian Eric Foner points out, the preservation of freedom was called upon to support slavery—the freedom to private property. It was also used to support abolitionism.[41]

In recent decades, however, some of the Left adopted a more "negative" view of freedom. A good example of the philosophical foundation of the moderate Left is the writing of Neil Gilbert, of the University of California at Berkeley, who discusses in several books how a new welfare state must reduce intrusion into American lives. The new American philosophy of government should enable people to do their own "rowing"; the welfare state of the 1960s simply went too far.[42] He calls for a renewed individualism in which Americans will reinvigorate their sense of personal responsibility.

Few will deny freedom a priority in American life. But it is so ambiguous and has been interpreted so broadly over the centuries that equality may well be more practicable, by which we may mean a level playing field, a more equal start. The challenges to maintaining the level playing field are always changing, as are the definitions of who—women, African Americans, Native Americans, gays—are even entitled to participate on an equal basis. Moreover, unfettered capitalism in the United States has been and can be abusive. We have too much history to think otherwise, from unconscionably low wages and egregious working conditions in the 1800s to stagnating wages since the 1970s for typical male workers to persistent gaps in wages between while males and black males or women.

Many on the Left believe these objectives can be met by preserving the spirit of the New Deal. Such efforts should include shoring up Social Security, expanding unemployment insurance, and preserving the Medicare program for the elderly passed under President Johnson in 1965. They also should include revitalizing some of the many financial regulations passed in the 1930s that have since been undone in part by the only Democratic presidents since Johnson, Jimmy Carter, and Bill Clinton. But invoking the specifics of the New Deal and the Great Society is inadequate in a changing time.

The New Deal failed to implement an efficient nationwide system of health care. But even beyond this gap, there have been many other changes in modern society since then that need addressing. Among the most important are the persistent stagnation of wages for several decades, the rise of both the two-worker and single-parent families, and the financialization and indebtedness of the American economy. Talk of merely reinvigorating the New Deal is too restrictive a view of government's purpose. It suffers from the easy and unchallenging reliance on proven successes of the past, and does not adequately address the present or the future. It does not preserve "positive" freedom in a new era, as liberals have tried to do in the past.[43]

The Myth of Laissez-Faire

What does our history truly teach us? It is not well-recognized, but America has had substantive social and economic policies in place since its earliest years.[44] One source of confusion is that contemporary economists, writing today in a time of substantial government spending, assume that a government's power is a function of how much it spends compared to the size of the economy. Tax revenues, largely from tariffs, excise taxes, and sales of government-owned land, were a small part of the economy in the late 1700s and early 1800s. Yet, clearly, under the first Federalists, presidents Washington and Adams, and even under the first Republican president, Jefferson, who was particularly skeptical of central government, the tools of government were wielded powerfully. These tools involved rules and regulations in land policies, trade, and internal commerce, as well as public investment in transportation and education. They included excise taxes and tariffs.

Much of the early Federalist history is well-known. Alexander Hamilton, Washington's treasury secretary, was determined to levy both excise taxes and tariffs on imports, invest in roads and other transportation infrastructure, establish a central bank, field a militia, and assume the debts of the Continental Congress. This was "big government" by the standards of the day. More important even than tariffs to Hamilton were subsidies for incipient manufacturing industries, of which he was America's arch-advocate. Aware of Adam Smith's "invisible hand," he undertook all these government interventions nevertheless—a set of measures, as one historian writes, "that Smith or any other protagonist of laissez faire would have found totally erroneous." (In fact, less popularly recognized, Smith had justified substantial government intervention for education, defense, and other areas.) Laissez-faire was a pleasant abstraction to Hamilton, to be respected but to be violated when necessary. As he wrote, "This favorite dogma, when taken as a general rule, is true; but as an exclusive one, it is false, and leads to error in the administration of public affairs."[45]

Many argue that the Constitution itself always allowed for federal government regulation and oversight in the famed commerce clause. We need not get into Constitutional controversies here.[46] What is clear is that America's early economy was highly regulated. Product prices were dictated by local governments, for example, and the quality of products was also regulated. Sales of products were legally confined to certain places and hours. Labor markets were especially unfree. Most American immigrants at the time arrived as indentured servants, even at the time the Constitution was ratified. The law provided they would remain indentured for seven years, unless set free by their masters.[47]

The myth of laissez faire, in contemporary discussion, apparently begins with Jefferson's victory for the presidency in 1800. Jefferson, a southerner and slaveholder, was after all in favor of nullification, the rights of states to override federal law. Jefferson was explicitly averse to expensive central government, federal indebtedness, and a central bank. He was an

admirer of Adam Smith's "invisible hand," and probably read
The Wealth of Nations years after it was published in England in
1776, having been first published in America in 1789. In Jefferson's mind, as historian Joyce Appleby puts it, "The modern
concept of self-interest gave to all men the capacity for rational
decisions directed to personal ends."[48]

A good government, Jefferson summarized in a letter during Washington's term, must be "a wise and frugal government, which shall restrain men from injuring one another,
which shall leave them otherwise free to regulate their own
pursuits of industry and improvement, and shall not take from
the mouth of labor the bread it has earned."[49]

Thus, the philosophy was set in principle, but Jefferson violated it in practice. The pragmatic basis of American prosperity and freedom resided in one fact, about which Jefferson did
not delude himself. Land was widely and inexpensively available. If you could own your own land, grow your own food,
have a safe abode, you need not be beholden to any man or any
ruler. Material self-sufficiency in an agricultural society of affordable land for the many was the source of freedom and
"happiness."

But laissez faire economic policy would not make this possible. Jefferson bought the Louisiana territory from Napoleon
for $15 million, which he agreed to borrow. He willingly de-
fied the Constitution's limits on his authority to do so without
congressional approval. In most other matters, he rigidly
abided by the Constitution. Given the importance of land to
America's material, social, and political objectives, though, he
did not stand on strict ideology.

But there was another critical choice Jefferson made. The
broad distribution of land he thought ideal could be accomplished only through government control and regulation. The
federal and state governments owned almost all the unclaimed

land at the start of the nation, and Jefferson was among the early political leaders who were determined to be sure the land was sold at affordable prices and was widely owned. To him, "the foundation of freedom in the United States rested on the abundance of its lands."[50] In fact, early in his political career, he proposed that his home colony, Virginia, give fifty acres of land to every citizen. Virginia would not implement his lofty goals in the state constitutional convention, though Jefferson had successfully rid Virginia of some of the feudal trappings of the Old World, including entails and primogeniture.[51] Entails prohibited land to be divided and primogeniture required that all land be passed on to the eldest son. Thus, in England, huge private landholdings could be retained under legal protection from the Crown.

Jefferson wanted to regulate the distribution of this new land. After the Revolution, the states confiscated the holdings of the Loyalists. Jefferson's state, Virginia, claimed the most land. When Virginia willingly ceded its land to the new Continental Congress, however, Jefferson demanded that it be done only if the land was sold according to the practices and principles he with others had conceived. His Virginia homesteading plan, which served as a guideline for the later federal territorial ordinances of the 1780s, required formal surveys and the division of land into sellable units of a limited size and at a fixed price. Thus, the influence of speculators, though hardly eliminated, was significantly reduced, and the ownership of land and its division into small plots was achieved.[52]

One historian computes that "about two thirds of white household heads owned land in places as different as Pennsylvania and Virginia. Such high levels of landownership persisted: about half the adults over twenty-one held land in 1798, and similar proportion owned land in early nineteenth century Tennessee and Ohio." There were still enormous land baronetcies—to which the great mansions on the upper Hudson River attest to this day—but three to four out of five workers who worked the farms in America owned them.[53]

This was a powerful use of government, even if land availability compared to the size of the population made low prices easier to implement. Federal laws controlled the sale of government land well into the twentieth century. Squatters were guaranteed low prices to acquire their land in the 1830s. The Homestead Act of 1862 controlled the sale of federal land for decades afterwards.[54] As the historian Frank Bourgin points out, the federal government was by far the largest owner of land in the nation, holding some 1.6 million acres at one point. It could have been a significant source of federal revenues.

Jefferson's famed advocacy of free trade and low tariffs was also grounded in practical needs, not ideological ones. Maintaining open markets and minimal tariffs would guarantee export markets for the sale of farmers' produce. It would keep the farmer strong and independent.

Jefferson's fear of big financial speculators was similar to his distrust of free-market speculation. To him, Hamilton's first Bank of the United States was a dangerous extension of the power of Eastern elites, and ultimately threatening to small farm owners. As for the new manufacturing industries, these too would eventually be controlled by elite interests, he believed. On this important point, Jefferson departed from Adam Smith's principal argument. For Smith, the source of wealth was the division of labor, which enabled farmers or manufacturers to increase output per hour of work and hire many laborers; it was the source of productivity growth.

But Jefferson could not ignore the rapid changes in the economy at the turn of the century. On balance, America prospered. "Never before," wrote Henry Adams in 1879 in his *Life of Albert Gallatin* (Jefferson's Treasury Secretary), "had the country enjoyed so much peace, contentment, and prosperity."[55] Markets for produce were growing and transportation was ever more available along the coast and into the interior. As the nation's income grew, farming was less a means of self-sufficient production and more part and parcel of a burgeoning commercial market. Farmers increasingly bought land on credit and had to cultivate and sell their crops regularly in geographically widening markets to meet their debt service. There was a clamorous demand not merely for free trade with Britain and Europe but also better roads and new canals in emulation of the great domestic transportation systems of Britain, France, and the Netherlands.

For all his disdain for government, Jefferson always sought to set aside federal land for schools. He was initially ideologically hesitant to use federal moneys for new roads, but by his second term he had changed his mind regarding the federal financing of roads. He even began to concede the inevitability of manufacturing.

If his view of the purposes of government could be summarized at all, it was best captured by a British writer, Thomas Cooper, in his book, *Political Arithmetic:* "Prohibit nothing but protect no speculation, at an expense beyond its national value. . . . Cut the cost of government, eliminate direct taxes and spend customs revenue on domestic investment . . . improve your roads, clear your rivers, cut your canals, erect your bridges, facilitate intercourse, establish schools and colleges, diffuse knowledge of all kinds . . . [56]

Jefferson had already approved the building of the Cumberland Road to connect the Potomac and the Ohio Rivers in 1806, which would become the largest public works project undertaken until the Erie Canal. He asked Albert Gallatin to prepare a comprehensive program of roads and canals to be implemented once the national debt was nearly paid off. Gallatin drew up an ambitious ten-year plan for the development of transportation that would cost a stunning $20 million, to be financed with bonds and paid off over time through tariffs and land sales. Jefferson believed a constitutional amendment was needed to authorize the spending. Perhaps he would have gotten it, but the embargo he imposed in 1808 on trade with Britain ended all such ambitious plans. "The planning that took place in Jefferson's second term of office remains to this day so little known," writes Frank Bourgin, "that the student of American history must marvel at this fact."[57] Bourgin focuses on the essential characteristic of American policy when it succeeded, which was when it responded to change willingly and constructively.

The Many Uses of Government in the 1800s

As Garry Wills writes about the early American historian Henry Adams, he "believes that the Republicans transcended both parties and party ideology itself, to become that most American of things—pragmatic. . . . Adams is right to say that Jefferson represents the best of the American people, since they are a pragmatic people."[58]

Madison, Jefferson's successor, recognized full well that soon enough land ownership in America would not serve the political and democratizing function it once did. Eventually, there simply would not be enough land and there would be no recourse but to encourage manufacturing. But could wage labor replace the farm as a source of personal freedom? Madison had his doubts. He worried America would one day be as populous as Europe.

After the War of 1812, Madison pragmatically signed into law a new tariff to protect domestic manufacturing, which in general Jefferson had opposed. He supported the renewal of a charter for a second national bank, again anathema to Jefferson. He would not fully support federal financing of internal improvements, however; like Jefferson, he argued a constitutional amendment was necessary.

It was admittedly difficult to imagine American going fully down the road of Europe, toward manufactures and vast new transportation systems. Adam Smith was taken only for what was useful to his various American readers. America had a touch of utopia to it. Even a Federalist like Noah Webster remained skeptical of the promise of a wage society. He captured the romance of America:

> A man who makes heads of pins or springs of watches, spends his days in that manufacture and never looks beyond it. This manner of fabricating things for the use and convenience of life is the means of perfecting arts: but it cramps the human mind, by confining all its faculties to a point. In countries thinly inhabited, or where people live principally by agriculture, as in America, every man is in some measure an artist—he makes a variety of utensils, rough indeed, but such as will answer his purpose—he is husbandmen in summer and mechanic in winter—he travels about the country—he converses with a variety of professions—he reads public papers—he has access to parish library and thus becomes acquainted with history and politics, and every man in New England is a theologian. This will always be the case in America, so long as there is a vast tract of fertile land to be cultivated, which will occasion emigrations from the states already settled. Knowledge is diffused and genius aroused by the very situation of America.[59]

Maintaining this condition was not the long-term path to a productive economy, however; it was unlikely it could be sustained. (Smith also was concerned about how wage labor would affect the population.) The clamor for new roads and canals grew louder. Farmers needed markets, workers needed jobs. Webster's romance did not apply to everybody. Gallatin's original 1807 plan attracted support after the Treaty of Ghent, which ended the War of 1812. John Calhoun, the powerful and persuasive congressman from South Carolina, was, along with House Speaker Henry Clay, the serious proponent of a new broad plan for internal improvements, which became familiar as "the American system." It was much along Gallatin's original lines.[60] But Madison could not get past his constitutional concerns and vetoed Calhoun's bill. Monroe was also sympathetic to federal development of roads and canals but he too hesitated, and made only modest headway on internal improvements.

In 1824, the Federalist John Quincy Adams, John Adams's son, was elected president, and was determined to expand the roads and canals. Bourgin calculates that under his administration the federal government spent more than in all previous administrations on roads and canals. But Adams never had broad political support for his programs and Andrew Jackson, who almost won the presidency in 1824 and was opposed to all such federal investment, was more than just nipping at his heels. With the rise of a new vitalizing democracy, and as more white males won suffrage and exercised their power in local and national elections, fear of central government rose. Jackson won the presidency in 1828, and stuck devotedly to his conviction that internal improvements were the province of state governments, not the federal government. The rhetoric of laissez fare was re-ignited under Jackson.

State and local governments started compensating for the lack of efforts by the central government. Frustrated by the Republican leadership in Washington since Jefferson's presi-

dency, many Republican followers of Jefferson and Madison
returned to their home states to implement new policies there
in response to growing opportunities and rapid commercial
expansion. Commercial pressure for new transportation systems was intense. Private investment could not support the
needs, largely because private investors did not have adequate
funds nor would any single one or even a consortium of them
reap all the gains. Turnpike companies went bankrupt right
and left, for example, but the roads provided benefits that
went far beyond the traveler.[61] They, like all transportation
venues, carried customers and workers, goods and services,
news and fashion, information and technology—all of which
expanded markets and helped business.

States had been supporting modest transportation projects
for a couple of decades. Frustrated by inactivity in Washington,
the Republican senator from New York, DeWitt Clinton, returned to his home from Washington in 1803 to become mayor
of New York City and later governor of the state, where he was
eventually responsible for initiating work on the Erie Canal.
The canal was easily the major public works project of the age
and was financed largely with state-sponsored bonds.[62] It took
many years to get the project started, in part because of the
war with Britain. New York State had in fact been building
roads for some time before it finally started the Erie Canal in
1817; it was completed eight years later. In addition, in this
period, New York's legislature made some twenty-eight major
loans to manufacturers, claiming "the establishment of useful
manufactures is clearly connected with the public weal."[63]

In general, the states borrowed far more than the federal
government until the Civil War, and invested several times as
much in transportation. Pennsylvania, Maryland, and Massachusetts, among others, made significant investments in
canals and other public works. On balance, state government

supplied more than two thirds of the money for the emerging nation's new canals.[64] They had invested substantially in other business, including local banks. And they were already supporting the railroads through land grants and with other financial subsidies. A Pennsylvania legislative document stated point blank that, "works of public importance deserve public encouragement."[65]

Local governments also issued hundreds of charters for corporations to do business. By contrast, such charters were more difficult to win in England, enabling government to restrain competition.[66] Similarly, the courts made major decisions promoting freer and more open competition among businesses, notably with the Charles River Bridge decision by the Supreme Court in 1837. The decision granted the right of another company to build a competitive bridge across the Charles. The courts overrode powerful and entrenched Harvard. This was in keeping with the Jacksonian anti-elitist spirit, which was more favorable to business competition than is realized.[67]

But the rise of laissez-faire attitudes under Jackson contributed significantly to America's philosophical skepticism of government and a diminished role for federal government until the Civil War. Jackson undid the Second Bank of the United States, distributing federal deposits to his beloved local banks throughout the states, and winning still more popularity with his growing constituency. Yet he defended tariffs to protect local industry and refused to side with southern planters in their attempts to "nullify" federal law. He sent federal troops to South Carolina to assert federal authority.

Jacksonian history is too complex to encapsulate here. Elite control of banking, for example, which he deplored, was not ideal by any modern standard. And even he could be a pragmatist at times. Still, it is hard to ignore the losses that could have been avoided in developing national infrastructure brought about by his vetoes of such legislation, and the loss of financial stability brought about by the demise of the bank. Some middle ground would have been valuable.

Support of primary education infused by the democratic spirit mixed with public investment successfully in these years. The Founding Fathers were generally committed to providing education for the people; Jefferson was one of the early leaders. But it was local government, particularly in New England, which encouraged and directed serious investment in primary schools through local taxation, mostly of property, beginning in the early 1800s. The public school system before the Civil War was the first major example of an income redistribution policy in America, because all property owners paid taxes and provided free education even for the poor. Originally, in fact, families were required to pay tuition for their children to cover part of the costs, but these charges were eventually eliminated. In 1827, for example, Massachusetts early on made it mandatory for towns with fifty or more families to provide free schooling, and other states followed the precedent.

By international standards, schooling in America was a remarkable success. More than half of the school age population was enrolled in primary school by 1850.[68] More specifically, 681 of 1,000 aged five to fourteen were enrolled in school; in Prussia, renowned for its education, the ratio was 732 per 1,000, only slightly higher; in England, the ratio was only 498 per 1,000 and in France only 515. France spent a larger proportion of its national income on education, but the United States spent as much per child. England was far behind in spending. The resulting literacy and rudimentary math skills contributed significantly to economic growth.[69]

■ ■ ■ ■ ■

After the Civil War, the nation entered a new age of rapidly advancing industrialization and large mass production and distribution industries. Big business was on the rise in America and became indomitable. Coal, steel, and machinery grew into enormous industries. Sewing machines, wooden wagons, cigarettes, breakfast cereals, chewing gum, frozen meats, processed sugar and flour, and store-bought clothing and linens were the great new consumer products. Large retail chains like the Atlantic and Pacific Tea Company flourished, along with department stores. Oil and gas were being used to light homes and cities. The steamship dominated the waterways and ever faster and more powerful trains and railroads that they ran on spread like spider's webs across the continent. Workers were drawn to the factories and mines, as were millions of new immigrants. The mills in Lowell once hired as many as three hundred workers, and were thought miracles of organization. In a generation, factories had thousands of workers. "Increasingly, wage labor, rather than ownership of productive property, became the economic basis of family survival," writes Eric Foner.[70] The profile of the nation became more urban, and the frontier literally and figuratively receded. Wage labor replaced farm labor in America.

Even as business grew at unprecedented rates—and the power of big business was never greater due to its size and financial wherewithal—the federal government had a critical part in the nation's economy. It was still the nation's greatest landlord. Through donations of land, partly under the influence of the rich financiers, of course, the federal government aggressively subsidized the development of the railroads; a reasonable figure is that it provided approximately half the financing for the revolutionary and highly productive national transportation system. This constituted a use of government where a subsidy was provided, just like a tax exemption or tax credit today. The government lost potential revenues by giving the land away rather than selling it.[71]

It is not clear that the private development of the railroads—grounded in intense speculation and resulting in frequent bankruptcy, and supported by government subsidy and plenty of pork barrel legislation—was ideal. It was a highly uncoordinated system, and to this day the national rail system is hardly a model of design. Germany managed its railroad development efficiently. But in the United States, government's participation in growth of the railroads was essential as a provider of capital.

Similarly, government used land to finance the first state colleges. These were started under the Morrill Act, passed in 1857, and extended in 1862. Lincoln was an advocate of the legislation. Federal land was granted to each of these educational institutions to finance themselves. If there wasn't enough federal land in a state, the university was granted title to land in another state, and the proceeds from the sale were to be used to sustain the college. The colleges were dedicated to the study of agriculture and the "mechanical arts," and the foundation was laid for one of America's exemplary achievements—the state university system. Cornell University in New York, the University of California at Berkeley, Ohio State, Pennsylvania State, Rutgers in New Jersey, Texas A&M, and the Massachusetts Institute of Technology, among many others, were started under this program.

The United States also expanded its postal system throughout the century. Mail was delivered routinely from city to city by pony express, the waterways, and eventually the rails. By the 1860s, major cities had post boxes on street corners; before that, people had to take their letters to the post office. The federal postal system in turn provided a steady demand for new transportation venues—roads, waterways, and the railroads—thus aiding in the development.

The nation's defense requirements created demand for new firearms, which made possible critical mass production innovations that America pioneered. With a guaranteed contract, the Springfield Armory created a system of interchangeable parts before the Civil War that enabled the company to divide the functions of making a single rifle among many workers, much as Adam Smith noted a pin could be divided into eighteen separate manufacturing tasks. British firearms were still hand-crafted laboriously and beautifully; American firearms were made rapidly, practically, functionally, and at much lower cost. This system became the forerunner of a mass production revolution in the United States, culminating in the thousands of interchangeable parts needed to put together one of Ford's Model Ts. It began with government contracts.

The donations of federal lands for the development of the railroads and the land grant colleges—direct investments in American productivity—are not recorded as government expenditures though, and thus escape attention as a government outlay, but the potential revenue from land sales that was foregone was enormous.

Politically, the great achievement of the Civil War, aside from ending slavery, was the establishment of an uncontested national government. Jefferson and Madison had favored a dominant role for states, whose governments were by their nature closer to the people. Though loyal to the principle of small government, however, Jackson as noted successfully opposed nullification.[72] For Jackson, points out the historian Thomas Bender, the Union and the states became concurrent powers. For Lincoln, however, the Union superseded the states.[73]

Lincoln changed the nation's direction markedly more, and ever after the "United States," once thought of as plural, was now a singular noun. Bender believes that Lincoln's determination to maintain the Union was partly influenced by the European revolutions of midcentury, in which nationalism became the means to guarantee the freedom and rights of the people.[74] Garry Wills persuasively concludes that Lincoln made equality the bedrock American principle in his speech at Gettysburg, and effectively made the Declaration of Independence the nation's main founding document, rather than the exalted Constitution. Now, as Lincoln re-interpreted it, America—all of it—was a nation that was "founded on the proposition that all men are created equal." This was not an extension of the past but a break from it; it was a changing nation. A strong central government, in Lincoln's view, was required to implement the principle he believed gave the nation its meaning.[75] As Bender and others have noted, Lincoln used the word "nation" five times in the Gettysburg address.[76]

Federal guarantees of equality were not passed under Lincoln but at last formally made during the Reconstruction, which was managed by the newly powerful federal government. The Fourteenth Amendment in 1868 endowed the federal government with the authority to ensure individual rights and the Fifteenth Amendment, passed in 1870, guaranteed voting rights for black men. This represented abrupt change in America. These were departures, writes Foner, from the central vision of the Founding Fathers:

> It is tempting to view the expansion of citizens' rights during Reconstruction as the logical fulfillment of a vision articulated by the founding fathers but for pragmatic reasons not actually implemented when the Constitution was drafted. Yet boundaries of exclusion had long been intrinsic

to the meaning of American freedom. Reconstruction represented less a fulfillment of the Revolution's principles than a radical repudiation of the nation's actual practice for the previous seven decades. Indeed, it was precisely for this reason that the era's laws and constitutional amendments aroused such bitter opposition. The underlying principles—that the federal government possessed the power to define and protect citizens' rights, and that blacks were equal members of the body politic—were striking departures in American law.[77]

■ ■ ■ ■ ■

A conservative turn soon dominated the nation as industrialization exploded, jobs became more available, some made fortunes, and opportunity seemed rife and there for the taking. The nation may well have tired of its battles for social justice as well. As an example of the turn in social opinion, the Fourteenth and Fifteenth Amendments were not adequately enforced for decades. By the 1880s, the Supreme Court limited their application, effectively affirming the right of states to enforce Jim Crow laws that mandated segregation in public places.[78]

As the economy grew, the way of life changed radically. The rise of new products and the replacement of farm work with factory work were accompanied by the rapid growth of cities. Twenty-six percent of Americans lived in cities in 1880 compared to 46 percent by 1910. The growing cities became centers for diphtheria, yellow fever, and tuberculosis. Working and living conditions could be abysmal, and life expectancy fell sharply in urban centers compared to rural America. Involuntary unemployment became a constant reality, though one often denied by many; the unemployed were thought indolent. As industrialization spread, the unions led sometimes violent battles for higher wages, safer and cleaner working conditions, reasonable hours, and the elimination of child labor. Social critics led new movements for reform of working conditions, housing, and health as life expectancy fell sharply compared to rural America.

But the federal government resisted efforts to develop new social programs, reflecting what seemed to be the balance of public opinion. At this time, such government intrusion was thought in theory to be counterproductive and in terms of values even immoral.[79] Freedom was the principle cited to justify the rise of poverty, disease, and squalor, but now it was redefined to justify limited government. "The dominant understanding of economic freedom was self-ownership," Foner writes of this period.[80]

By the 1890s, even as its economy became the largest in the world, Americans were deeply confused and divided. In 1893, Frederick Jackson Turner attributed the disarray to the closing of the frontier. If oversimplified, his thesis did reflect a breach in the American promise. In that same year, the nation fell into a deep recession that lasted several years. Unemployment in industry averaged 20 percent during what became known as a depression. But such was the state of ideology at the time that no public works program to maintain employment was considered in Washington, nor was any other relief of unemployment considered. Laissez-faire doctrine was dominant more or less until the turn of the century. British philosopher Herbert Spencer's popular theory of social Darwinism excused poverty as the natural state of a battle for the survival of the fittest; those who were poor deserved it. Eugenics became the spurious, pseudoscientific justification for government-sponsored sterilization of people of undesirable genetic origins in many states.

Government as an Agent of Change in the 1900s

We cannot easily conjure up a truly felt sense of how insecure life was in America in the 1800s, even though average wages rose over time and opportunities were typically more available than in the Old World. Immigrants kept coming to the New World for economic reasons, though the flow decidedly receded during severe recessions. As jobs disappeared on farms, and the frontier receded, there was no refuge during the many deep cyclical declines of the nineteenth century, when unemployment and bankruptcy rose dramatically. Old age became a scourge in an industrial era where the elderly could not simply remain in the family home until their deaths. Unemployment, now prevalent, could no longer convincingly be attributed to indolence; there were too many Americans in these circumstances. New cities made miserable the living conditions of the poor and low-wage workers. In 1890, Jacob Riis graphically photographed the squalid life in New York City in his popular work, *How the Other Half Lives.* By the early 1900s, muckraking was thriving. In the pages of *McClure's Magazine* at this time, Lincoln Steffens focused on the demanding and often corrupt life in cities from St. Louis to Minneapolis, Philadelphia, and New York and Ida Tarbell targeted John D. Rockefeller and his practices in the same pages. Upton Sinclair's popular novel, *The Jungle,* castigated working conditions in the meatpacking industry.

As last, the political pendulum began to swing the other way. A new kind of industrial development of big business and urbanization had changed America. In the minds of a growing number of Americans, suffering and unequal opportunity could not be dismissed so easily as the inevitable and justifiable consequence of further economic growth. Social Darwinism was being displaced by the social gospel that preached communal responsibility. The meaning of freedom was again shifting.

Still, federal government spending, if much larger than before the Civil War, remained a relatively small proportion of the nation's total income in the new Progressive Era, some 7 or 8 percent of GDP until World War I. Rather, the Progressive Era that began in the late 1890s and carried forward until the 1920s emphasized new regulations and a broadened democracy at the federal level, but not many new social programs.

In this period, amendments to the U.S. Constitution were passed by the nation's state legislators that provided for the direct election of Senators, who were until then appointed by state legislatures; they approved of progressive income taxes, and provided women suffrage. The fearsome panic of 1907 led to a financial crash so threatening that it at last gave rise to national support for a new a central bank. J. P. Morgan and his friends famously saved the day in 1907, and the Federal Reserve was created in 1913.

In the late 1880s and 1890s, new federal regulations of commerce between states were already being undertaken, if tentatively. The antitrust actions by the federal government began (though weakly) in the 1890s but gained strength in the early 1900s, culminating in the break-up of Standard Oil and the American Tobacco Company in 1911. In the presidential election of 1912, all three candidates were essentially progressive in one degree or another: Theodore Roosevelt, who had broken from the Republicans, Woodrow Wilson, the Democratic candidate, and the incumbent, William Howard Taft, who actually broke up the oil and tobacco giants in 1911. In this period federal meat inspections were established and Wilson, who won the presidency in 1912, passed an eight-hour maximum day for railroad workers in 1916.

But it was at the state and local level where new social programs were put into place. Spending on health programs, city
services, and education rose rapidly. The state and local governments were active investors in the nation. It was an erup-
tion of active government, in fact. They built many new parks.
They developed high schools, for which demand increased
rapidly as business evolved and needed better educated workers.
In 1910, 10 percent of Americas graduated from high school;
by 1940 more than 50 percent did, and 70 percent of high
school age Americans at least had attended.[81] This represented
a remarkably swift rise in America's educational standards.

The local governments invested substantially in health. Aside
from saving lives, what some called the "age of sanitation"
made it possible for cities to grow without the constant threat
of disease, becoming in themselves major sources of wealth
and innovation.[82] Germ theory had become internationally accepted and government financed new research and dispensed
the invaluable vaccines.[83] The city governments developed
elaborate and expensive sewer and water systems. More than
two thirds of Americans in big cities were connected to public
sewers by 1909. By 1915, almost all big city dwellers in America had access to sanitary public water systems. As a result,
water-related diseases like typhoid fever were reduced and
even eliminated. One estimate is that the public moneys spent
on water systems produced social returns of 150 percent.[84]

In addition, myriad new regulations protecting workers, retirees, and consumers were implemented by the states. In
1896, New York State required that all children be vaccinated
against smallpox. The states passed many new safety and inspection regulations over products. (Some states banned cigarettes and liquor, for example.) State governments established
workers' compensation and regulated working conditions.
They passed legislation for minimum wages and maximum

working hours for women, and passed child labor laws. Most states paid widows' pensions by the early 1930s. The cities franchised or regulated the new electricity and gas utilities. Few alive in the early 1900s could have imagined a nation with minimal government attention to these vital matters. A changing economy required government attention, whatever the political philosophy that justified it. Meanwhile, the nation prospered.

During World War I, the rates on the new income tax were raised substantially from a maximum of 7 percent to a maximum of 77 percent in 1918, and income taxes were extended to lower income people as well. The income tax financed one third of the cost of the war.[85]

America raised its income taxes substantially in wartime, but typically lowered them afterwards. In the 1920s, the tax was repeatedly cut. There was a decided return to the laissez-faire attitudes that characterized the nation after the Civil War, and demands for new social programs were typically cast aside. For example, Americans went to war in Europe in the early twentieth century, the nation was widely reminded, for the sake of individual liberty, and regulation of business would supposedly undermine that. In fact, regulation was said to be unpatriotic. Socialist publications were prohibited from using the public mails and the conviction of the antiwar activist and socialist Eugene Debs, who ran for president from jail in 1920, was upheld. Unions were often categorized as socialist sympathizers, thus enabling business to gain public support for undermining them in the courts with the help of local political officials. Union membership declined significantly in these years. In the name of freedom of labor, minimum wage and child labor laws were struck down by the Supreme Court. These abrogated freedom, it was claimed, because they prevented people who chose to work for these companies from doing so. During the war, anger had been turned on immigrants from warring nations and this opened the door after the war to policies to restrict immigration from southern European nations in the 1920s. Much of the harsh treatment of dissenters was essentially a continuation of censorship and antiespionage practices put into effect by Wilson himself during World War I.[86]

One especially disturbing symbol of the change was that the federal government took no action in this period against lynching of blacks, at that time all too common in the South. The worst of the national disgraces was the resurgence of the Ku Klux Klan in the mid-1920s, gaining strength even in the North. But even the progressive sympathizers of the period did not for the most part include the plight of blacks in America among their concerns. Blacks would have to wait yet another generation for justice.[87] New Deal legislation would also neglect African Americans.[88]

In this period, the nation's economy grew rapidly, however, serving as proof to advocates that the negative freedoms advocated—liberty from the state—were beneficial. It was an extraordinary business era. Arguably, commercial innovation had never been as intense. By the start of the decade, Ford's Model T was produced so efficiently that costs fell to affordable levels. Electricity spread to the factories, cities, and the homes. New consumer electrical products were also mass-produced efficiently, including the record player, the refrigerator, and the telephone. Factories were widely electrified. Chemical companies made remarkable innovations, and agricultural productivity rose rapidly with the development of artificial fertilizers, seeds, and insecticides. Hollywood and its talkies were born. And the financial community grew and prospered, largely unregulated by government. Banks, rife with conflicts of interest, sold their own company's stock to savers and lent money prodigiously to risky borrowers, investors in stocks borrowed on margin at irresponsible rates, and stock prices rose to unsustainable heights.[89]

On average, real wages rose in these years, but income inequality also grew and later data suggest the large body of workers did not benefit commensurately from the rapid growth. Because prosperity did not reach deeply into the economy, the suppression of rights, the scapegoating of ethnic Americans, and the rise of the Ku Klux Klan probably became attractive outlets for working class frustration. As women went to work, men were also threatened by their new dress and liberal social mores. "The idea of freedom," wrote an economist in this period, became "an instrument for looking backward."[90]

Resistance to the uses of government, despite the early advances of progressivism, had always been more intense in the United States than in comparably wealthy nations. Public pensions provide a useful example. Prussia had established a public pension system the late 1880s, and by the 1910s so had most European and all the Scandinavian nations. The United States was the last of the major nations to do so, establishing Social Security only in 1935 during the Great Depression. The payroll tax was at first 2 percent of wages, shared equally by worker and employer.[91]

But even in the Roaring Twenties, there was a progressive undercurrent of activity. Immigrants demanded their American right to civil protections. Angry muckrakers continued to write about income inequality, business abuse, and financial corruption. Some had already warned that the financial markets had expanded out of control by the late 1920s, and that prosperity was resting on a fragile foundation of speculation and corruption—that much of it was mere froth. But it required a market crash in 1929 and countless people losing their savings in failed banks, as well as frightening levels of unemployment in the early 1930s, to convince the nation to adopt new policies for a complex, industrialized economy. During the Depression, thousands of banks failed, the unemployment rate rose to 25 percent, and industrial production fell by half at its low point. Probably two in five were unemployed at one point or other. Faith in the laissez-faire philosophy of the 1920s was undermined—creating a new but deep national skepticism many observers thought would be permanent. But, the groundwork for further progressive reform had long been laid in America, starting with populist reaction in the late 1800s, running through the presidencies of Theodore Roosevelt and Wilson, carried further by state and local governments, and proselytized by immigrants, unions, and muckrakers in the 1920s.

Under Franklin D. Roosevelt, a remarkable mixed bag of new regulations, institutions, and spending programs was attempted in a spirit of experimentation. The Federal Deposit Insurance Corporation administered the new federally guaranteed insurance on bank deposits, designed to prevent runs that undermined the banking system from 1930 to 1932. The Securities and Exchange Commission was given oversight over the brokerage community. The Glass-Steagal Act separated investment banks and commercial banks, and established regulations on the interest banks could pay on deposits. The Federal Reserve was also reorganized to attend more efficiently to monetary policy.

A minimum wage act was passed, as was legislation to enable unions to organize more easily. Meanwhile, the government raised income taxes, and a serious public works program was established to build the nation's infrastructure. Social Security was created at last in 1935. There were reactions and disagreements over these measures. Roosevelt's programs, including Social Security and the new labor laws enabling unions to organize, first had to overcome considerable dissent by con-

servatives in Congress, and were threatened by Supreme
Court decisions later in the 1930s. But eventually, in a show-
down with Roosevelt, the Court relented on these two matters. National health insurance was high on Roosevelt's agenda
as well, but it never made it to the floor of Congress, in part
due to the intense lobbying efforts of the American Medical
Association.[92] By 1938, Congress was balking at the breadth of
Roosevelt's programs. He stepped back from his boldest ideas.

But government spending did not reach levels as a proportion of the GDP that would have on their own lifted the nation
out of Depression. The surge of military spending in 1941 and
1942 of nearly 10 percent of GDP led quickly to full employment, however, by stimulating demand for goods and services
and by providing military and civilian employment to millions.

After World War II, almost all economists feared a reprise
of the Depression. It was hard to imagine what could replace
all the lost military demand. But the opposite occurred. After
a pause in 1947, the economy grew as rapidly on average as it
ever did before, and the incomes of most working Americans
grew faster than ever before. The progressive turn of policy,
despite a resurgence of antigovernment sensibility, did not
deter growth. Nor did higher income tax rates, which were
raised by Roosevelt during the Depression and were raised
again to record levels during World War II, where they remained for more than a decade. The highest tax bracket reached
approximately 90 percent, where it remained until 1964. To
the contrary, bigger government seemed to go along with ever
faster growth. Roosevelt had proposed a G.I. Bill of Rights in
1943, among other things, to provide aid for veterans to go to
college and to buy a house. Congress raised objections, but in
1944 the G.I. Bill was passed. By the late 1950s, half of the re-
turning sixteen million soldiers financed college or other training programs as a result. Millions of mortgages were guaran-

teed.[93] The nation was thus directed in a particular way. The Marshall Plan under President Truman, and named after the secretary of state who strongly advocated it, provided billion of dollars of aid to rebuild Europe.

Dwight Eisenhower, as a former president, incurred the ire of the Republican right wing by proposing to expand Social Security coverage to another ten million workers—to include farm workers and professionals such as teachers, accountants, and dentists. He also increased benefits. Eisenhower said that it was simply clear that not all could save enough for retirement.[94] Eisenhower also advocated the development and federal financing of a national highway system. He had strong support from the major auto companies, of course, and the bill passed in 1956. By the late 1950s, 90 percent of all homes in America were reachable by road, and often by highway. It was an explicit case of national government coordination and investment that deeply influenced the development of the nation into a new geography of suburbs, based on cheap gas, cheap property, and mostly free roads.

In these decades, the federal government financed and administered the antipolio vaccines. In the wake of the Soviet launch of the first space satellite, Sputnik, Congress passed the National Defense Education Act, providing billions of dollars of annual grants and loans to support higher education, technical training, and other educational programs. Young people were further spurred to go to college. The National Institutes of Health, as an extension of late nineteenth-century government investment in health research, were expanded dramatically after World War II, and accounted for a high proportion of medical breakthroughs. Research and development (R&D) was undertaken in many federal agencies, not least the Defense Department, where the Internet had its origins. The federal government accounted for most of America's R&D, in fact, through the 1960s, topping out at 67 percent of all such research in 1963.[95] Many economists contend that such intense research efforts account for greater American economic superiority in these years than any other single factor.[96] The Supreme Court under Eisenhower, led by Johnson's appointee as chief justice, Earl Warren, ordered that public schools be integrated.

In the 1960s, President Johnson passed Medicare and implemented his War on Poverty, including health care for the poor under Medicaid. Regulatory changes were significant, and included landmark civil rights legislation, which protected voting rights for blacks, ended Jim Crow laws once and for all, and forbade gender and racial discrimination in labor markets. Other regulatory reforms involved cigarettes, packaging, motor vehicle safety, consumer credit, and the expansion of the authority of the Food and Drug Administration.

Between 1948 and 1970, the share of spending in GDP by the federal, state, and local governments rose from 16.5 percent to 27.5 percent, nearly eleven percentage points. Most of this increase was in social expenditures. Yet productivity, wages, and overall GDP grew very rapidly, as noted. What is the complaint then in light of all this success? It is hard to escape the conclusion as noted earlier in this section that government did not hurt but significantly helped economies to grow.

The Economic Benefits of Government

Why so much success? Let's summarize as we near the end of Part I. Few economists disagree with the theory that some measure of public investment in infrastructure, education, and health care is necessary. Because public goods such as roads and schools benefit society overall more than any individual or business, such investment would not have been adequately undertaken by private firms. Adam Smith, Milton Friedman, and many centrist and liberal economists have been of a single mind about the value of this investment. The debates occur over how widely government should support such efforts. Yet even Friedman, in *Capitalism and Freedom,* argues that government support is required for primary education, roads, and the poor.[97]

Far less frequently discussed is the fact that government can be the focus of needed and useful coordination. When railroads used different size track (gauge), government was needed to standardize them. By organizing communities to use a single public water system, government creates economies of scale for such a public good. The highway system was an immense act of coordination that probably couldn't have been attained through a private network; there is no example of one in the world, in any case. The system of international trade and currency valuation is a government-led example of coordination.[98]

Similarly, regulations can and often do make economies work better. They can make information about products and services more open. They can reduce corruption, monopolistic pricing, and anticompetitive policies regarding research, innovation, and new products. They can temper financial speculation, which distorts the flow of capital toward inefficient uses and can often lead to costly corrections and serious recessions, as occurred yet again in 2008.

Some regulations can be poorly administered and reduce economic efficiency. Others will outlive their usefullness; they should be pruned and streamlined over time. But other regulations will be a short-term cost to business that the nation chooses to bear for quality of life and even a better economy. Maintaining the safety of products that consumers cannot judge for themselves is an example; but the safety and effectiveness of products also makes consumers more confident buyers of products. Environmental regulations adopted in the early 1970s have probably been costly to all of us, but they are a cost we bear for cleaner air and water and the diminution of global warming. It is no cause for alarm that regulations have multiplied as the economy supplies so many more goods and services to the people. As economies change and grow more complex, it is only natural that more oversight is needed.

At the still more liberal end of the political spectrum, some economists will argue—though not the American mainstream—that programs that help raise and make wages more equal, such as laws that facilitate union organizing, minimum wages, and equal rights, may well aid economic growth, not undermine productivity, by creating demand for goods and services, and also reinforcing faith in workers that they will be fairly rewarded for their effort. If high taxes allegedly reduce efforts, surely unfair compensation should do the same. Fair compensation should improve effort. This book is not the place to develop this suggestion more fully, but it a highly reasonable argument.[99]

One of the key benefits of the larger post–World War II government, if in some quarters still a controversial one, is also that it makes the economy more stable. Well before Keynes's work during the Depression there were calls for government spending to create jobs and support incomes. Massive public works projects that reignited economic growth, such as Baron Hausmann's rebuilding of Paris, are common in history. But in the post–World War II era, such activities gained new theoretical justification from Keynes's theories. Both Keynesian liberals and some Friedmanite conservatives accepted, to one degree or another, that fiscal and monetary policy—deficit spending by the treasury or the adjustment of interest rates by the central bank—could help avoid or ameliorate recessions and thereby raise the rate of growth over time.[100] A large government is itself, despite conservative arguments cited earlier, a bulwark against rapidly declining spending. Unemployment insurance, Social Security, and government employment itself are stabilizing factors.

If the size of government truly and directly caused the inflation of the 1970s and contributed demonstrably to slower economic growth, it would be reason for concern. But we have seen that it did not in the United States, and nations with far larger governments have produced neither more rapid inflation nor substandard levels of income for their citizens. The public goods and social programs of many countries—from Sweden and Norway to France and Germany—are significantly more generous than America's.

Resisting a Pragmatic Government

One of the ironies in America is that government was used aggressively in the face of persistent laissez-faire rhetoric. The constructive government policies were reactions to changing economic conditions and requirements, new expectations for a decent life, and evolving attitudes about the rights of all kinds of people. Some of these policies were radical by any historical standards, in particular early in the nation's history. The distribution of land and the end of feudal practices such as that entails, as well as the investment in free education, were remarkable departures from the past.

There is a natural human tendency, noticeable even among the best of historians, to assume that a nation's history turns out as well as it could have in the end—the end being the point at which the observer takes note. Mistakes may have been avoided along the way, but we made it this far, didn't we?

But a laissez-faire philosophy took its toll. Had there not

been frequent ideological resistance to the uses of government, the nation may have done better both economically and in terms of the influence and maintenance of its own ideals. The free-market development of the railroads in the second half of the 1800s was probably not an efficient use of government land. The resistance to a government health care system has likely cost the nation enormously in the quality of care and its efficient distribution. Public transit has been neglected. The nation has been unable to turn its attention to government-directed alternative energy programs partly due to its philosophical bent. In the 1970s, after oil prices were dramatically raised, the hundreds of billions of petrodollars in the hands of producing nations were loaned by private banks to susceptible developing nations, ultimately ending in financial catastrophe a decade later. Public management and coordination of the flow of these dollars may have been more efficient. The Clinton Administration, despite hundreds of billions of dollars of budget surpluses, felt it could not get new public investment passed. The capacity of government to coordinate activity across local, regional, and national boundaries, to create economies of scale in public goods and in a global world, to serve as the only possible agent to address new regulatory and coordination needs— these go almost unrecognized.

Today, America requires the reinvigoration of government. It is now a nation of relatively low wages and little support for the rising numbers of two-worker and single-parent families. The financing of adequate health care and pensions is jeopardized. The education of its young is often failing. Its highways and infrastructure need updating. And international competition rises rapidly and inexorably.

The nation is also increasingly run by a generation of people too young to have experienced the successful economy of the 1950s and 1960s when government was a full, equal, and appreciated partner in growth and equity. The new generations have not actually experienced a robust economy and an America that believed with some justice in what it could do rather than what it could not do. The mythology of laissez-faire is alive and continues to do damage.

It should come as no surprise that government is enlarged over time as the economy becomes more complex, new products proliferate, and expectations rise. Critics cite growth of government as a cause for alarm with little attention paid to the needs of a changing, intricate, and complex economy and society. This is the very nature of modern progress. Change requires government—good government, surely, but there is no good government without faith in government itself.

PART II

·················

How Much
We Have
Changed

The History of Change

BOOKS LIKE *Future Shock* or magazines like *Wired*, which claim
that change is now faster than ever before, are misleading. The
evidence does not at all support the snappy conclusions. To the
contrary, rapid change confronted America time and again
over two hundred and fifty years, usually arriving in explosive
spurts. Many conditions were necessary to produce rapid
change, including: large and growing markets and increasing
exchange of goods and services; the innovativeness of capitalism; a literate, skilled, and increasingly educated population;
financial markets to encourage savings and channel it towards
investment; the expansion of international trade; scientific dis-
covery and technological invention; a new humanism and
sense of personal possibility; more efficient transportation; and
the rise of democracy.

These conditions culminated in the industrial revolutions of
the late 1700s and early 1800s. Integral to all these was government. Increasingly, economic historians, though not necessarily public policy or macroeconomists, recognize that none of
these conditions, including technological advance or increasing

savings, was alone sufficient to produce the scale of change that occurred. The sources of economic growth are difficult to sort out and the subject of numerous controversies.[1] But what is clear is that America's history, beginning in the 1770s, was coterminous with most of these revolutionary new conditions and that consistently rapid change throughout its history was a result.

The period following the War of 1812, known as the Era of Good Feelings because of the amity between political parties, was one of the earliest examples of explosive change. Farm exports, cotton in particular, grew rapidly; the price of land on which cotton was grown in Alabama and elsewhere soared to heights that were eventually unjustifiable and even absurd; financial speculation went unchecked; food, spices, and textile products became widely available, much of these imported, and helped change the way people lived; and an incipient manufacturing base began to take hold. In just a few years, beginning in 1815, the nation changed remarkably, yet by 1819, much of it came crashing down.[2] The economic debacle that ensued affected almost all industries and regions in the nation, thus making the Panic of 1819 the first modern financial crash, and leading in turn to the first modern recession in American history, insofar as it affected essentially the entire economy. The recessionary impact cast a shadow of fear over the nation. The scenario would be repeated with regularity for the next one hundred and twenty-five years, where financial excess and financial bust were constant characteristics, and recession, bankruptcy, and unemployment the inevitable painful consequences. The fear of collapse, unemployment, and personal failure persisted over the course of the century.[3]

American history is similarly replete with examples of social and cultural transformations stimulated by new products, which typically arose and helped cause and sustain economic booms. The so-called New Economy of the 1990s was hardly one of a kind or, for that matter, one of a century. The cotton gin had an enormous impact on America's early nineteenth-century economy. Advances in water mill and canal technology followed. The telegraph was invented in the mid-nineteenth century, reducing communication time radically. Arguably the most influential of all new devices for its utility in both the home and the factory was the mechanical sewing machine, which became widely available in the mid-1800s. Cheap kerosene and natural gas eventually brought many more hours of daylight to American lives as well, and expanded commerce in the cities by the late 1800s. The advanced steam engine, the steel furnace, and the railroads were among the great new commercial developments of the mid-nineteenth century. Early mass production machinery gave Americans cheap cigarettes, matches, chewing gum, and breakfast cereals. There were rapid improvements in services productivity in retailing, transportation, and communications with the development of the department store and retail chains, the railroads, and the telegraph. Retail chains like Sears and the A&P lowered costs and changed the nature of shopping, for example. As for the development of new consumer products, it would be hard to match the pace of change in the 1920s, with the proliferation of cars and electricity in general, the latter giving rise to the mass production and wide ownership of inexpensive record players, telephones, refrigerators, washing machines, electric sewing machines, radios, and other means of entertainment such as the cinema.[4]

The pace and dimension of changes in health care beginning in the late 1800s, well before contemporary times, were also remarkable—arguably more remarkable than today. As noted, the development of sanitation, sewage systems, and public water works by local governments radically changed life in big cities in the early 1900s, as did diphtheria treatments and small-pox and other vaccines. Sulfa drugs became available in the 1930s, penicillin after the war, the polio vaccines in the late 1950s. Agricultural productivity improved at unprecedented rates with the innovations of the chemicals industry beginning in the 1920s.[5]

In the 1950s, we had the revolutionary advent of television, which changed news, entertainment, culture, leisure time, and consumer advertising in one Promethean burst. Air conditioners made development of the South and Southwest feasible. Inexpensive and durable plastic products of all kinds entered lives at every level. Jet plane travel became frequent. Enormous cargo ships made commercial transport much cheaper. Perhaps the greatest change was that the new highway system gave rise to the expanding and eventually dominating suburbs.

I don't like the rubric, New Economy, but if we must adopt it, then America had many such new economies in its history. The new products of the latest New Economy can be compared on equal footing with, but do not exceed their predecessors in influence over American life. The Internet is a marvel with widespread consequences for communications, knowledge, politics, and even personal freedom. But so were the telegraph, the telephone, and the television. That the Internet can perform new and different tasks does not make it a more indelible or powerful presence. These predecessors did new things as well compared to their predecessors; we simply now take them for granted. Earlier periods may well have been more transformational, in fact.

New drugs and medical procedures like angioplasty or hip replacements are wondrous but they are not necessarily comparable to the medical breakthroughs of earlier times. The iPod sweeps the nation, but so did the Sony Walkman, and before that the now seemingly lowly but then culturally significant and modern transistor radio. The original radio gave rise within a few years of its commercialization in the early 1920s to hundreds of radio stations. At the time, it had almost as great an impact as television had in the 1950s and 1960s; half of all people in the 1930s got their news from the radio.[6] Good new sneakers have enabled the middle-aged to walk longer and farther, but think what the invention of eye glasses did for the middle-aged and elderly four or five centuries ago, or what the clock did for civilization in general.[7]

New products are simply not an adequate measure for distinguishing the pace of change in the last two hundred years or for claims that they in themselves vary the standard of living. The myopic appeal of "future shock" is the glamorous and self-important claim that now we are different. We are, however, always different.

Explaining the shift in the American economy from manufacturing to services—a ubiquitous piece of conventional analysis—also does us little analytical good in trying to assess the causes, impact, and extent of change in contemporary times. This evolutionary fact—from a farm to a manufacturing and then a services economy—is merely the bare bones of the matter. Take a historical example. An agricultural economy, which included rising farm productivity with the development of rudimentary tools such as deep plows and horseshoes, as well as increasing knowledge about fertilizer, did not confer on the French people in 1800 the same degree of individual sovereignty as it did on the early American people. If it had, perhaps the French Revolution would not have been so vindictive or self-defeating. All agricultural economies are not the same, nor are all manufacturing economies.

More pertinent to U.S. economic evolution than the breezy, abstract characterization of an agricultural economy was that the ratio of land to the population in America was high compared to the Old World and that surplus farm production was readily sold to Europe, where demand for foodstuffs in particular was strong, even desperate. Thus, access to land ownership and independent farming, along with worldwide demand for wheat, grains, cotton, and tobacco, made the American farmer a special historical personage, not the agricultural economy per se. The American political system, as examined earlier, supported access to farmland for ordinary ambitious people, and democracy was partly an outgrowth of it. This never eliminated poverty; not everyone could get the capital necessary even to buy relatively inexpensive land. But ownership was unusually widespread and changed the nature of life in America. The shift to a manufacturing economy also had particular rather than merely general consequences in America. As manufacturing waned, wage labor became a larger part of America's production in the 1800s, but it could not replace land as an equivalent guarantor of individual political autonomy.

Thus, a manufacturing economy arrived with a completely different set of political implications and presented new challenges to America's commitment to individual rights. Workers in America did not merely have to make the transition from the farm to the factory, which is how it is often simply put in retrospect. The new manufacturing economy, which today's economists too readily assume was historically analogous to an agricultural economy, created a fundamentally different social and political environment than the one that preceded it. The nature of society had to change to assure that the rights of the so-called common man were protected in an economy that profoundly reoriented the relations of power among individuals.

America—the American government, to be exact—accomplished this, but only with remarkable determination, struggle, and frequent failure, the last partly, I would argue, because of ideological constraints imposed on it. Its commitment to an egalitarian ideal was often tested. The nation adapted through the inventive, courageous, and persistent uses of government as much as and at times more so than through the adaptive and innovative energies of business from which government policies and institutions cannot be truly separated. Note that this does not diminish the essential place and wondrous contribution of business, but raises the place of government as a full participant in economic history.

Moreover, America did not only become a more manufacturing-oriented society as it evolved from a farm society, but it also became a more commercial society. There is a distinction here. This evolution was already taking place in the farming years. A social and cultural environment of goods and services, advertising and marketing, freight and personal transportation, marked the new nation—not simply manufacturing. Means of communications were more available and not only daily news or business orders but also technology, managerial ideas, and business values spread more rapidly. There were now town squares and main streets with gas lights, new modes of marketing and advertising, and a deepening belief in public education. Marketing became an American business passion, led in particular by the young tobacco industry and innovator James Duke. The labor market radically changed as many new and different kinds of jobs became available, not all of them paying well by any means. And market relations—those between consumers and business, employers and employees, readers and advertisers, business and suppliers, land buyers and land owners, renters and landlords, and savers and borrowers and bankers—became key new ways in which people related to each other. Thus, a commercial set of relationships seeped into American life, and competed with the traditions of family, child rearing, church, and local community.[8]

A market society created opportunity and concomitant

stress. One simply had to know more to get along—to read, to make change, to do basic arithmetic, to travel, and increasingly to get a good job and perform well at it. Failure in a land of allegedly equal opportunity was easy to attribute to one's inabilities or inadequate character, however unjustifiably. The nation took a long time to acknowledge in the dawning manufacturing age that unemployment itself could be involuntary, even as personal failure became palpable due to the frequent loss of jobs, business bankruptcies, and the inability to pay off personal debt, the result of the regularity of crashes and recessions.[9] Industrial and commercial society, as well as urban expansion, brought ill health and abhorrent living conditions. All this was not merely an extension of an agricultural economy to a new sphere, the manufacture of goods—factory jobs simply being an equal replacement for farm work. Society was fundamentally transformed.

A full life, in the minds of Americans, increasingly required access to consumer goods, to vaccinations and clean water, to education and transportation, and to varieties of entertainment. Personal failure in a society of opportunity was read in one's clothing and housing and transportation and experience, as was success. In turn, expectations of a rapidly rising standard of living took root, so successfully did incomes rise and the economy grow. The income adjusted for inflation of the typical American worker of a given age kept rising, if cyclically.

Today, observers say that Americans can confidently make the transition to a service economy, just as we did from an agricultural to a manufacturing society—as if there were a fixed and immutable law of economics involved. It is irresponsibly simplistic. The mechanics of the alleged law, appealing to the way of thinking of many economists, is that even though some good jobs are lost, on balance, the United States will do as well or likely even much better as it transforms into

a services economy, just as it did in the transition to a manufacturing economy when similar fears were generated among
farmers who had to move to the cities to work in the factories.
There may be many low-end jobs, but there will probably be
more good jobs—that is, those with longevity and decent pay.
Contrary to myth, we are told, services also provide good jobs.

This is the abiding assurance of capitalistic growth, and faith
in a precise repetition of history—that is, services are to manufacturing as manufacturing was to agriculture—is taken by
some as inevitable. To take but a single example, written with
customary arrogance and scorn for those who may think otherwise, one informed and literate observer on a blog writes:

> It is true that employment in manufacturing is decreasing.
> Employment in farming has fallen from 20% in 1940 to 5%
> today, and yet we are wealthier than ever. From 1983 to
> 2002, well paid managerial and skilled-professional jobs
> have increased from 23.4 percent to 31.1 percent of em-
> ployment. With continual advances in robotics and au-
> tomation it is inevitable that manufacturing will go the way
> of farming, where much of the reduction in employment
> was also due to technological and methodological ad-
> vances.[10]

Would that it had been that simple or easy.

Advocates of this simple explanation of American advance
badly neglect the central part government had in making more
equitable the painful and uncertain transition to a manufacturing economy in the first place, and the creation and enhance-
ment of the basic conditions of growth—an ever-more educated population, efficient transportation, communications, a
body of law, health systems, and the coordination of the assets
of an increasingly complex economy. They also underestimate
the many contours of change described above. A services soci-

ety and a high technology economy, which goes hand in hand with it, in fact, will require far more education—thus more costly investment in human capital. Will output rise commensurately to provide an adequate return on the cost of evermore education? Will adequate jobs therefore be created to pay back those who spent money and took time to attain more education? The assumption is that they will. But it is an assumption, hardly an inevitable fact.

■ ■ ■ ■ ■

Other changes are underestimated as well. There are new demands over time to include more people under the protection of American rights: to include fully women, people of color, immigrants, and now gay people. As medicine advances, it becomes more expensive, but we believe that most are entitled to rising levels of basic care. As the baby boomers age, there will be fewer workers to support the pension and health care needs of the aged. Growth increasingly pressures the capacities of the planet to provide resources and remain environmentally sound.

A society of high energy costs may well need a different kind of transportation system that requires serious and centralized or at least regionalized coordination—the equivalent of the design of the interstate highway system. It may require better and new kinds of housing and planning of location and development to minimize travel time as distance entails more cost. The list goes on and on, and government has a central part in such coordination.

Given the advance of knowledge generally, there is a reasonable argument to be made that the pace of useful innovation may increase. Nothing is so generative of new ideas as the large size of the existing supply, and as that grows larger, it should yield more. Yet such advance may depend on the continuation of rapid economic growth as well—that is, an expanding GDP. It will require the conditions to reward and nurture new ideas materially, if the past is any model at all of the future. Growth creates those conditions: the demand for new goods and services and therefore the profit to reward innovation. A changed world today creates many requirements that cannot be anticipated and that do not have precedents, but the continuation of reasonable material reward will probably remain a necessity.

The attention paid to globalization and the New Economy does not fully define the quality and breadth of change today. Ask a typical person—or even a policymaker or media commentator—about change and it is likely the term "globalization" will roll off the lips with simple certitude, soon followed by reference to the Internet. But in the late 1800s, the global flow of capital was large and was the key to financing the nation's railroads, among other advances. The international flow of goods was also intense in this era. Trade resumed after World War II, having been interrupted by two wars and the Great Depression, and American business began to move offshore rapidly in the late 1950s. The nation started importing aggressively from lower wage nations in the 1970s. As we shall see, the failures of the economy and the loss of good jobs began before modern globalization or the Internet had allegedly closed its grip on the world. Globalization is real and an ongoing concern, but it is not an all-encompassing description of how America has changed in the past thirty years.

■ ■ ■ ■ ■

Truth usually lies in the particulars, and as I repeatedly write there is danger in the easy appeal of glib overgeneralization. Economists do not have a seriously cogent theory of economic growth, in my view, at least not when they try to reduce causal factors to a mere two or three, and given that economists too are embedded in historical trends, abrupt change almost always catches them by surprise. Yet abrupt change has been the rule, not the exception, since the beginning of the Industrial Revolution in the late 1700s, and most likely change was more rapid than is recognized in various localities in earlier eras as well, though it is unlikely that it was equivalent to the pace of modern change in the industrial times of the last two hundred and fifty years.

The nature of change in the American economy, and the resulting change in how Americans live, again took a new and not adequately recognized turn in the early 1970s. Most important, beginning then, the economy started to grow significantly more slowly than it had over any similar period of time since the end of the Civil War—thus, since true industrialization began in the United States. In other words, GDP, the nation's total income, grew significantly more slowly than in most of its past. This was not widely understood. Typically, analysts argued that the economy slowed only compared to the rapid rates of growth of the immediate post–World War II period. This is not true. The growth of government tax revenue also slowed, putting pressure on finance, but this was claimed to be irresponsible spending rather than the result of new circumstances.[11]

The proximate cause of the slowdown was the inability of business to improve productivity as rapidly as in the past. Productivity, which is the measure of business output of goods and services per hour of work, is what enables economies to grow faster than the working population. The more that is produced per worker, the more money that is potentially earned per worker. Productivity increases are therefore the necessary source of a sustained rise in the standard of living. The sharp slowdown in growth represented a break in America's economic history that was never fully appreciated.

This slowdown persisted through the ups and downs of business cycles from 1973 to 1995, and partly but not solely as a result, wages did not rise significantly in this period. For many, they stagnated or fell. But the causes of the productivity slowdown were never agreed upon by economists. The slowdown began in the inflationary 1970s and very early 1980s, when inflation reached 12 and 13 percent and interest rates soared to 20 percent or so, but slow productivity growth persisted in the 1980s as inflation fell. Some analysts in the 1970s also attributed the slowdown to increasing trade, and the usurpation of traditional American markets by Japanese cars and electronics and European consumer goods and machinery. The United States had its first trade deficit in 1971, and by the end of the decade the annual deficit was large, and by the 1980s well above $150 billion. A related difficulty was a persistently high U.S. dollar, which made American industrial exports expensive compared to foreign competitors. The high dollar was not a result of the relative values of imports and exports so much as it was due to the special place the dollar had in international finance. The world wanted dollars because people, business, and governments trusted that these dollars would hold their value. They were willing to lend to American government and business at lower interest rates because the value of the investment would not fall in terms of their own currencies. This kept interest rates lower than they otherwise would have been, enabling Americans to borrow at prodigious rates. The higher dollar however, made American exports more expensive, and undermined the nation's manufacturing industries and the good jobs they once provided.

The proportion of Americans with manufacturing jobs started falling some time ago. These lost jobs were the sorts that provided a middle-class living to workers with only high school education or less. Increasingly, new technical and social

skills were needed for manufacturing jobs, and new high technology industries then required college graduates. The high
dollar also put these high-school workers at a persistent disadvantage.

At the same time, the American economy had also become
more a "new office economy" than a manufacturing economy.[12] Finance and banking, health care services, marketing,
sales, consulting services, communications and media, and retailing grew rapidly—not only high technology industries.
Employment in these service businesses often required a college degree, not only because many jobs were sophisticated,
but also because, unlike factory jobs, they required face-to-
face contact with clients and customers, as well as commu-
nicative and decision-making skills. Services gave rise to many
low-skilled and low-paid jobs as well, especially in retailing
and fast food.

In general, wages grew much more slowly than in the past.
At the same time, they grew, beginning in the late 1970s,
steadily more unequal, after three decades of remarkably equal
advance. Those who were educated and of a certain socioeconomic status did better. Increasingly though, even many of the
more privileged did not do as well in terms of the rate of growth
of the standard of living as they had in the past. Ultimately, slowing wages coupled with rising costs of key services, notably education and health care, placed pressure on the family unit. There
were two responses—coping mechanisms. Spouses went to
work and people saved less or borrowed substantially against
their assets. The American economy became financialized—in
short, ever more indebted.

Despite this variety of new factors that affected all Americans, the media and political focus was placed on new technologies that revolved around computers and semiconductors.
The problem was that new technologies were supposed to en-

hance productivity, and thereby maintain a rapid rate of wage increase, but for more than twenty years there was a pervasive slowdown in the growth of output per hour. New theories arose to explain the slowdown in productivity, the most popular of which among economists was that major new technologies usually took time to be incorporated and developed.[13] This was an overgeneralized and insupportable view of historical developments, in my view, but it was widely accepted. It is dangerous example of metaphorical thinking. A threshold, a critical mass, or in today's parlance, a tipping point, is somehow reached, even though it cannot be defined explicitly or forecast. It is thus not like the critical mass of nuclear fission, upon which the analogy is partly based, where the quantity of fissionable material needed to set off a chain reaction is calculable. But the loose borrowing of this metaphor from nuclear physics apparently gives such thinking credibility. Why wasn't the so-called critical mass reached in enough smaller markets to raise productivity at least gradually over time? The implication is that the use of technology had to be economy-wide before it began to show up. Historians claimed that the productivity consequences of electrification followed a similar pattern, but this too was loosely drawn history. Too many factors, not all of them technological, go into the mix of productivity growth. The historical analysis advanced to back up the theory of critical mass was at best ambiguous, and at worst merely an attractive and important-sounding metaphor.

There are other factors that can better explain tepid productivity growth: international competition, a remarkable and still little understood surge in new products for niche markets (which undermined economies of scale); floating exchange rates, which made international trade less certain; and the rise of low-productivity industries like finance and retailing—many services, in general. However, economists came up with no widely held consensus about what caused the slowdown.[14]

But the productivity slowdown abruptly reversed in the mid-1990s after more than twenty years of perplexing disappointment. Under President Clinton, productivity grew rapidly again, and incomes for all groups, not just the educated, started to rise with it. Some inevitably argued the computer revolution at last reached its critical mass. But there were other factors. The Federal Reserve, long concerned with inflation, at last stopped adopting restraining monetary policies (essentially, high interest rates) to suppress inflation. They were aided in their looser policy by President Clinton's 1993 tax increase, which helped hold down the federal budget deficit, providing an anti-inflationary margin of error lest the Federal Reserve let interest rates fall too low. There was also rampant speculation in stocks and, on an individual basis, in housing, which supported personal and business borrowing to support spending and investment. In my view, there was also a return of mass production economies of scale as demand grew and new companies, from Intel to Microsoft to Wal-Mart, dominated industries with mass market products and methods the way U.S. Steel, G.M., the A&P, and later IBM once did when U.S. preeminence was unchallenged. An economy of niche markets since the 1970s, in which productivity was difficult to raise, again gave way to an economy of mass producers and distributors by the 1990s, much like the older, traditional American economy of the Industrial Revolution.

Such economies of scale were in the past the source of enormous productivity increases, and they were again. "American manufacturing firms and their technologies not only were resources and capital intensive, but operated at much greater scale than did their counterparts in the United Kingdom and on the Continent," write economists Richard Nelson and Gavin

Wright of the first American industrial age.[15] Now, scale could be exploited again by manufacturers such as Intel, Microsoft, and Cisco but also services companies like Wal-Mart.

Despite globalization, the flattening of the world, and new technologies which, economists had claimed, meant workers needed a college education, incomes for all categories, rich and poor, educated and not, grew satisfactorily in the late 1990s boom for the first time in more than two decades. This golden period was short-lived, however. The stock market crashed in 2000 and business spending did not grow robustly. Despite military spending on the Iraq War and deep tax cuts, a recession drove up unemployment rates again. Meanwhile, tax cuts contributed to a widening budget deficit. The climb out of recession was disappointing in terms of the number of jobs created and the growth of wages, even as productivity and business profits rose rapidly. Unlike the Clinton years, wages did not rise with productivity and a new and disturbing economic relationship posed serious questions to economists.

From 2001 to 2007, wages discounted for inflation did not grow at all—unprecedented in any post–World War II expansion.[16] Mainstream economists generally argued that markets work well enough so that workers will always participate fairly in rising productivity. But beginning in 2001, productivity increases have been largely siphoned off into profits, not wages. In fact, it is likely productivity increased to an important degree because the wage bill was suppressed as increasingly powerful CEOs tried to raise profits to support their weakening stock prices (and thus their personal wealth based on stock options) through hard-driving wage bargaining, rising imports from low-wage nations, and increasing offshoring. Only in 2006 did wages start to rise somewhat faster than inflation, yet a typical family's income as late as 2007 was lower than it was in 2000. By 2007, wages turned down again. Even more disturbing, the more rapid growth in productivity ended by 2003 and rates of growth of this most important of all economic variables returned to the slower rates of the twenty-year period between the mid-1970s and the mid-1990s. As of this writing, America is entering a slowing and perhaps recessionary economy that will cause wages to fall even before they ever seriously rose.

■ ■ ■ ■ ■

What is clear is that so much ground was lost since the 1970s that the exuberant performance of the late 1990s could not fully compensate for the decline. We need not fully understand the causes of the slow growth of the economy to discuss and deal with its consequences. These consequences have changed the way we live. For all the media attention to the eye-catching generalizations about globalization and high technology, the true nature and extent of change has been underestimated.

In the 2000s, Malthusian fears became a vivid possibility. Evidence increased that industrialization had despoiled the environment and that future growth may be permanently impeded by global warming. Penalizing growth by making energy more expensive or allocating it more stringently appeared to be the only answer. The increasing demand for energy and the Iraq war combined to push oil prices to new record levels. There had been many warnings of environmental abuse in the past, when relatively few discussed outright government investment or coordination, especially in the major media, but now it appeared it could no longer be neglected. Global pollution, along with the rising costs of medical advance and the future costs of an aging population, added serious obstacles to a rising standard of living.

Yet, as noted, a larger base of ideas than ever before is likely to inspire the development of more new ideas at a faster pace.

These may well include technological answers to climate change and environmental limits. The growing size of an educated workforce also reinforces the likelihood of more rapid technological advance. This may over time be enough to support adequate economic growth as resources become depleted, and without unconscionable environmental damage. But it won't occur without other conditions that nurture economic growth yet maintain equitable rewards and access to decent lives, for these are also sources of growth. And it is unlikely they will occur without active government participation as a source of investment and coordination.

When we look back, it is too easy to conclude that government responded to past change because needs then were so obvious. But when a society is undergoing such change, it is not well aware of how deep and lasting a transformation may be. Needs are unambiguously obvious only with the benefit of hindsight. The last thirty to forty years has produced underestimated rates of change in America in many areas, and overestimated rates of change in others. The most profound change is the damage to the standard of living, and the consequent pressure on the family and the American way of life. There has been a concomitant rise in the demand for more education and sophistication. More than any other single fact, a rising standard of living has defined the American history of the last two hundred years. It is the central foundation of the way the nation is governed and the way its social and political institutions have been formed. When it is damaged, much else changes.

The New Challenge to the Standard of Living

I'd like to demonstrate and discuss this one basic change in detail because it has been so influential over American society.

What do I mean by damage to the standard of living? To put it most simply, the U.S. economy no longer raises the incomes of workers the way it once did. In particular, the failure has profoundly affected the fortunes and prospects of males. For three decades, a large proportion of men have lost ground in terms of weekly pay and benefits and a majority have failed to meet even very modest expectations of a rising standard of living. A majority has been unable on its own to maintain a family in a reasonable middle-class way of life, given the new costs and new demands of a contemporary age. A majority has not seen its income grow as rapidly as the costs of education, day care, health care, drugs, or public transit. Among males, some have done very well, and a large gap in incomes has opened up between well-paid workers and the rest.

Women's compensation has risen over these decades at moderate but not exuberant rates. Like men's, however, it has become highly unequal and for most women remains well below men's income for those of the same age and education. For American men with only high school diplomas, the standard of living has declined significantly over the course of a generation.[17]

I would like to put this as clearly as possible, because it is neglected by both the Right and the Left in America. There has been a sociological and psychological schism in the nation across two great divides. One divide is between male and female. The ability of men to make an adequate, esteem-enhancing living since the 1970s has been severely damaged. This did not occur solely because women made more money; they still make inadequate livings in comparison to men. And, even as women enter the labor market at a prodigious rate, there is still ample evidence of gender discrimination. Indeed, this may well have contributed to the divide. As women are discriminated against, they are more easily hired at lower pay to do the same work as men. Men's personal status meantime was deeply undermined by the stagnation of their wages.

It is one of the fine achievements of the time that women could find work in greater numbers, but an adequate economy would have been raising most boats, even if perhaps raising women's wages faster. In fact, the gap between men's and women's wages remained high. Was there substitution between men and lower-paid women? As one commentator in the 1980s correctly put it, men have been "stiffed" in the last third of the twentieth century and so far in the twenty-first. But, in fact, so were women. This issue was discussed momentarily in the late 1980s and early 1990s then rapidly forgotten in the rather short boom of the late 1990s, but it has persisted and helps explain a lot of American frustration that has manifested itself in so-called cultural battles over religious and social values and disenchantment with government in general.[18]

The other divide is by education—and by extension, class circumstances. The plight of men and the plight of those with only a high school diploma of course overlap. On average, those who go only to high school can no longer make it in America, by which I mean they no longer have ready access to the middle class. And those who only go to high school are disproportionately from families whose parents have lower incomes to begin with, families in which parents also have no more than high school diplomas, and from families of color—all of which means America has also developed a palpable class divide.[19]

As regards men, even those with a college education are not on average doing well. There is a growing divide within this group as well. Median incomes of college-educated men have risen by only 10 percent or so since the early 1970s. Over thirty years, a rise of 10 percent in median income is inconsequential; it is essentially stagnation. More to the point, for periods of twenty and twenty-five year intervals since the late 1960s, these median wages and salaries were flat to declining, which is a long period. The more typical increase for males over thirty to thirty-five-year periods since the Civil War would have been 30 or 40 percent to more than 100 percent. Moreover, compared to the rising costs, as noted (and I will repeat this theme time and again), of education, health care and other key services, these incomes have fallen behind. This is why we must be clear. Men in general have been harmed in the economy. Male high school graduates have been severely set back. The great advantage of the American manufacturing economy at its height was that, with the aid of government labor protections and organized labor, it could provide a middle-class life for high school graduates, and men in particular. That is no longer the case. Meanwhile women, though they have closed the gap, have not adequately caught up.

This raises the same question once raised when industrialization evolved from an agricultural economy of widespread land ownership. Could manufacturing jobs pay well enough and be secure enough to become an adequate substitute for the security of land ownership in early America? The answer turned out to be yes, but only with much political turmoil, lost personal independence, and the active participation of government. In the 1800s and early 1900s average wages rose for two reasons: rapid productivity growth and substantial government regulation and social transfers, including minimum wages, maximum hours, worker safety laws, public pensions (Social Security), and a variety of necessary public goods that were free to the user, including roads and highways, water and sanitation systems, vaccines, and of course high-quality public schooling. Now we face another set of shifts in the economy that is as hard to define and which will assuredly not follow a simple fair path without diligent oversight.

Note a key example here of the failure of government today: Americans must now go to college and ideally graduate school to raise prospects of a middle-class life, but this amounts to a significant new cost in America. It is the cost of four or even six years or more of education. Keep in mind, however, there were often before new costs in America—in the early 1900s, the cost of four years of high school and in the 1800s the costs of primary school. It was government that provided the solution in both cases, however. Kindergarten through twelfth grade in America was financed as a public good, free to the individual, the cost borne by the public largely through property taxes (and the early per pupil tuition payments were eventually eliminated). This is how it should be, because the gains were broadly social as well, not simply individual. Now, however, government has not risen to the occasion of providing college for all who choose to go.

■ ■ ■ ■ ■

Let me present the most relevant wage data gathered by the Commerce Department and the Bureau of Labor Statistics, in particular because there is so much denial about the poor performance of the economy over the past three to three and a half decades. We should begin by looking at wages overall, discounted for inflation, which are known as real wages. I will almost always mean real data when I refer to wages, salaries, and compensation in this book. The most oft-cited data are the hourly and weekly real earnings of production and non-supervisory workers. These exclude the 20 percent of American workers who are managers, such as business executives, or are professionals, such as lawyers and doctors. They include workers in most jobs, as well as most public servants, such as teachers, fire, and police personnel.[20]

The average weekly earnings of such workers, discounted

TABLE 2

Real Average Weekly Earnings of Production
and Non-supervisory Workers (2005 dollars)

1973	$581.67
2005	$543.65

Source: Mishel et al., *The State of Working America*
2006/2007, p. 119.

for inflation, was $580 or so in 1973 and only $545 or so in
2005. Over the entire period, the average weekly wage never
attained again its 1973 high. The hourly wage performed only
slightly better. The hourly wage finally reached the 1973 level
by the end of the 1990s, but it has barely risen higher. Thus,
roughly speaking, the average American production or non-
supervisory worker was able to buy fewer of the goods and
services that constitute a typical annual package of such products compared to the average person thirty years earlier.

This declining average wage does not mean that you, or
your parents, cousins, or children, were necessarily unable to
buy more in 2005 than in 1973. What a decline in the average
wage tells us is that an average worker in 1973 made more
than an average production worker in 2005. For example, we
can infer that a production worker aged thirty-five with a high
school diploma and a steady job typically earns less today, after
inflation, than someone of the same age with a similar background did in 1973. But what we can also infer is that even as
individuals got more experience and earned higher wages and
salaries, the gains were not nearly as robust as in the past and,
in addition, many workers did not earn more at all.

Twenty percent of the work force—typically the better educated, higher-income workers—are not included in this data set. Had they been included, the average would have risen. But even when the better-off workers are included, the average wages did not rise nearly as fast as they did in the twenty-five years after World War II.

So let's turn our attention to another government data series that includes 100 percent of workers. It measures the hourly wage. This time, we won't measure the average, because it is pushed up by the gains of very high-income workers, but rather the median. The median is the worker in the fiftieth percentile, the one who makes less than 50 percent of all workers and more than the other 50 percent. When economists talk about a typical worker, they usually are referring to the median. The average, unlike the median, can be skewed deceptively higher if incomes at the top of the range are very high, as we know they were.

In 1973, the median worker (out of all male and female workers in America) earned $12.99 an hour, discounted for inflation (in 2005 dollars). In 1989, the median worker earned only $13.13. So, up to this point, the median America worker earned only a few pennies more than the median American worker sixteen years earlier, in so-called real terms. The median wage of all workers rose robustly in the late 1990s, and in 2005 the median hourly wage was $14.29. Still, including this increase, the median wage was up only about 10 percent over thirty-two years. By contrast, it had doubled—up 100 percent—in the previous twenty-five years.

This number includes all workers—male, female, all races, and all educational backgrounds. For men alone, however, median wages were down. In 1973, the median male wage was $15.76; in 1989, $15.35; in 2005, $15.64. The typical male worker in 2005 was thus earning less than the typical worker

TABLE 3

Falling Median Hourly Wage for Men

1973	$15.76
1989	$15.35
2005	$15.64

Source: Mishel et al., *The State of Working America*
2006/2007, p. 122.

in 1973. Judging by what historical data we have, the median wage of men never before failed to make an advance over thirty years in the past.

Let us also consider actual men, not just a median in one year compared to a historical median twenty or thirty years earlier. One way to get a sense of how actual people did as they gained more experience over time is to derive data from another series, which includes not only wages but most other kinds of income, including government social transfers. From this data, produced by the Census Bureau, we can find how a median male worker of a certain age did, say, in the 1970s, compared to a median male worker ten years later and ten years older. It is not precisely the same worker, obviously, but it is a reasonable indication of the performance of actual American men over time. We are comparing median workers in every decade.

The results are informative, and show how poorly many males have done. A median male worker who was forty-years-old in 1964 would have earned 25 to 35 percent more by the time he was fifty in 1974. But a median male who was forty in 1974 would have earned essentially no more in 1984, despite ten years more experience and training. The forty-year-old in 1984 who turned fifty in 1994 would have earned only 5 percent more; the forty-year-old in 1994 who turned fifty in 2004 would have earned only 8 percent more.

TABLE 4
Median Income for Males by Year and Age (2006 dollars)

Age	1954	1964	1974	1984	1994	2004
30	23,432	31,849	37,808	33,442	30,402	33,801
40	25,907	36,110	45,446	45,406	41,310	43,226
50	24,372	33,749	44,300	45,448	46,995	44,865
60	20,443	27,449	35,968	36,092	36,424	41,936
65+	8,109	11,316	16,727	19,315	20,516	22,555

Source: U.S. Census Bureau, Historical Income Tables: Table P-8. Age of people, all races, by median income and sex: 1947 to 2006.

The same relationships hold for younger workers. As one turned from thirty to forty in the 1960s and 1970s, incomes rose for the median worker by 40 to more than 50 percent. In the 1980s and 1990s, the increase in these, typically the most productive years, rose by no more than 20 percent. In other words, not only did men no longer earn what their father's earned a generation earlier at similar ages, their increases were significantly less as they got older. We can further infer that a high proportion of males—probably between 30 to 40 percent—literally lost ground in a decade's time as they fell from one percentile to a lower one. At best, the majority either lost ground or gained only marginally. Only the younger workers saw more than marginal increases because they started from such a low base at their first jobs. But these gains, as noted, were much lower than they were earlier in the ear. And younger male entry workers in the early 2000s were doing far less well it turned out than their peers a decade earlier.[21]

With this data, we can begin to draw some conclusions. More than half of men who were forty or older at any point beginning in the 1970s had a seriously disappointing economic experience—marginal increases or actual declines in income adjusted for inflation. Those in their thirties did far less well than their parents. At best, a worker who was in the middle of the pack throughout his career earned only slightly more over time. Meanwhile, women were earning more, but still not as much as men, and those near the top of the income scale experienced a much faster pace of increase than those in the middle. At least the incomes for most cohorts of women rose, but those at the top of the income scale rose much more rapidly.

It was heartening and significant that women's wages and salaries rose over these years, as noted. If some of the hiring came at the expense of men, it was nevertheless also encouraging that so many women found work, which gave them greater independence and a welcome control of their lives. Barriers were breaking down in many categories of work. However, women's wages remained disturbingly low and unequal, and this made them exploitable; gender discrimination was simply still evident in the wage data. Women earned on average less than four fifths of what men did, even after incomes rose.

Regardless of the moderate progress for women, however, men's social and family roles and their sense of themselves were seriously challenged by the stagnation of their incomes, even if men arguably made more than they otherwise would have in earlier decades because women were socially dissuaded from working. The general way to keep one's head above water in the last third of the century was therefore to be married to a working spouse as well, or to borrow aggressively. If we turn to family income data, we can see how much of a difference it made to marry another worker. Consider the median data for family incomes. Among couples, median family income since 1973—those in the middle of the distribution—rose only for the group whose spouses worked. In 1973, median family income for a married couple with a spouse in the workforce was $56,114. In 2004, it was $76,814. Most of the gain was due to

TABLE 5

Median Family Income by Family Type, 1973–2004 (2004 dollars)

	Married couples		Single family head	
	Working spouse	Spouse at home	Male-headed	Female-headed
1973	$56,114	42,409	39,560	21,349
2004	$76,814	42,221	40,293	26,964

Source: Mishel et al., *The State of Working America 2006/2007*, p. 55.

the extra hours worked by the spouse. For families in which only one person worked, median income was $42,049 in 1973 and $42,221 in 2004—essentially no rise over three decades. For families with single parents, those headed by a male experienced no appreciable increase in median incomes over this period. For those headed by single mothers, incomes rose but remained very low—some 60 percent of those headed by a male.

Families with two workers reached about 45 percent of the work force. But, as we can see, the typical members of the other 55 percent of families—those with one worker, or with only one parent—made no gains at all at the median and a high proportion of these lost ground over the years.

How meager were these gains by historical standards? Between 1947 and 1973, family incomes generally doubled after inflation. Those were especially strong decades, but it is reasonable to conclude that family incomes never grew as slowly over an entire generation since the Civil War as they did between 1973 and 2004, and for many sub-categories, let's keep in mind, there was no increase at all. Most of the damage was done between 1973 and 1995. Median family incomes regardless of family composition hardly rose at all over this period. In the latter half of the 1990s, incomes rose rapidly but, as noted, they fell again in the early years of the twenty-first century even as the economy measured by GDP grew at a formidable pace. Family size declined between the 1970s and the early 1990s, but the income gains were still modest even if we adjust for this reduction in the number of children per family. Family size has been stable for well more than a decade. Moreover, when families have fewer children, it may well be because of new financial insecurities; such sacrifice in number of children is effectively a reduction in the standard of living, which goes unmeasured.

Fairly constant gains in the standard of living have characterized life in wealthy countries since the dawn of the Industrial Revolution more than two centuries ago. Before that, there was often reversal or stagnation; historically, this was considered a failure and a concomitant characteristic of the decline of nations. The eighteenth century in The Netherlands, for example, was largely a century of stagnation after a century of rapid growth. The Dutch did not literally regress in terms of GDP per capita, they kept up.[22] But keeping up was not good enough. Society was fraught with problems, even if the average stabilized, and various groups suffered more than others. Britain soon overtook the Dutch and overpowered them economically. Now, there has been essential stagnation in America for a large proportion of families for a very long time, even as key costs of education, health care, and drugs rise rapidly.

The American dream, as economists Isabel Sawhill and John Morton point out, is not simply about striking it rich. It is about a persistent climb in incomes adjusted for inflation even when a son or daughter did comparable work to his or her father or mother. Americans just kept doing better. Economists Frank Levy and Peter Temin call this mass upwards mobility—absolute upward mobility. For men, it stopped in the late 1960s.[23] To repeat, as Sawhill and Morton point out, a typical male in his thirties makes less (discounted for inflation, as always) than his father likely did when he was in his thirties, discounted for inflation.

The Broad Threat to the American Promise

Still, the meaning of income stagnation for many Americans is in dispute, even among economists. In the current general discourse about what ails the nation, little is made about the impact of the historically weak labor market as a source of political frustration over a generation. One reason is that people still only associate truly poor times with palpable poverty, hunger, disease, and very high levels of unemployment. I know the reader may be wondering: "But in the past, we were starting at a much lower level. By the 1970s, we were at a much higher standard of living and little progress from such a high level does not mean we have a crisis or even a serious problem."

However, today, if deprivation is less palpable or immediate, it is nevertheless real and punishing. There is much poverty in America even though the poverty rate is now lower than it was forty years ago. Poverty also afflicts African Americans and Latinos far more than it does white people. Reliable studies show that the rate of child poverty is higher in America than it is in any other rich nation.[24] If we see people in a clean tee shirt and jeans, and even plump in the tummy from eating too much, we might not imagine that there is social deprivation. If they have a nice color TV, a DVD player, and a microwave oven, we think they must be fine. No matter that they do not have decent health insurance, and many have no health insurance at all, which studies clearly show diminishes the quality of lives and also reduces life span. No matter that co-pays and co-insurance, as well as premiums are rising, and people are probably increasingly neglecting their health. No matter that they eat and fill up and are indeed plump, but they may have an insidious disease that will not affect them for another ten years, such as Type 2 diabetes. No matter that they have a DVD player but their kids do not have a chance to get beyond high school or community college, the man of the house may have spent time in prison, or that they have found themselves in a societal and economic rut from which their children will have great difficulty escaping. No matter that the family must hold two jobs or at least the equivalent of a job and a half to make ends meet, with enormous pressure on family life and the ability to attend adequately to children. No matter that so many must live with a quotidian sense of uncertainty about jobs, rent, their children's education, and for many of color especially, the fear that a family member will wind up in prison. Many more Americans today wake up with less hope and a greater sense of anxiety over their future.

No matter, finally, that the male of the species has lost self-esteem because he is unable to support himself or a family. More economic equality among the sexes should be admired and highly desired. It is not merely a matter of the justice of equal pay for equal work, but it also helps to create equal power within personal relationships, which we know can otherwise be abused. The stagnation and loss of male income is nevertheless a cause of considerable and often shamefully unspoken anxiety about roles in the family, about care-giving, and providing an adequate environment for raising children. Such change requires support. The stagnation and decline of male incomes raises levels of frustration and fear that may well cause people to seek a scapegoat through political victimization and the narrowing of individual rights and social programs.

In truth, many Americans eat poorly (it is far cheaper to do so), have inadequate medical care, and get inadequate educations. People in America live significantly less fulfilling lives as a result of failed government response: they are less healthy, often grievous, less interesting, and often live shorter lives than need be. For many, making an adequate living means that both spouses work, which puts pressure on the family and the children that once was far less prevalent. For single-parent families, a growing proportion, the pressure is intense. Meanwhile, adequate health care depends on having a job—it is too expensive to afford privately for the large majority. Uninsured people in America live lives with greater fear than others of getting a disease or being hit by a car, or even the less-than-likely possibility of being hit by a falling tree branch.

In America today, a much higher proportion of Americans go to jail than ever before. A higher proportion must go to a public hospital for treatment, and these uninsured receive treatment too late. A high proportion of preschool children get no care giving, and the care giving many get is largely unregulated and with untrained personnel. Corporations, despite the recent wealth, have revamped pension plans, shifting from guaranteeing benefits to requiring workers to contribute savings themselves, and manage the investments as well. People are deeply indebted, and a higher proportion now go bankrupt.[25]

Some new evidence now suggests that relatively few Americans are able to rise from the socioeconomic level into which they were born than once was the case. Is all this a national tragedy? The very fact that many think it is not suggests that they have accepted an age of national limits.[26]

Meanwhile, some in America do unprecedentedly well. One study concludes that the top 1 percent of earners makes an additional 10 percent a year of the nation's personal income than they did twenty years ago. Very roughly, that comes to an additional $500,000 an earner per year in the top 1 percent than if the income distribution had been the same as it was in the 1980s.[27] Americans do not resent others becoming rich, let's concede. But such riches raise to impossible heights national standards of adequacy and undermine confidence in fairness and equal opportunity.

If American do not worry about how much other people make, there is evidence that relative positions in society matter. We are talking about dashed expectations and the broken promise of ever improving standards of living, and the complex psychological issues concerning happiness. A relative decline in status, many studies now show, takes a mental and physical toll.[28] The less privileged find themselves ever farther behind. Change has made all this more difficult. To be part of society requires higher levels of education, social presence, and skills than ever before.

When I was a young man in college in the late 1960s, Americans talked not merely about work but about *meaningful* and *interesting* work. Not anymore. There had long been the expectation in America of steadily improving standards of living. Now any job is a good job, goes the conventional wisdom, because it imposes discipline and enables someone to leave a federal or state assistance program. Some commentators seem to believe that the standard of living in America rose seriously only after World War II—a historical aberration.[29] They are wrong; the American experience has been decidedly different. Even in colonial years Americans lived better, judging by health records, than their Old World peers; they ate well, had fewer diseases, and were decidedly taller on average. As we know, the accessibility of land—not universal, to be sure, but plentiful by the standard of the day—was an early boon to American optimism and the impulse for democracy. Notions that all men were equal emanated from such access to land and the narrowing of income distribution in those early years compared to the Old World. "In no case," writes historian Gordon Wood, and to repeat a theme from the earlier section, "was the overall situation of property-owning in America comparable to that of England, where more than 60 percent of the population owned no property of any kind. Freehold tenure in America was especially widespread, and freehold tenure, said William Knox bluntly, 'excluded all ideas of subordination and dependence.' . . . Both eighteenth- century observers and historians ever since have repeatedly commented on the egalitarian character of colonial society. America, it seemed, was primed for republicanism."[30] Thus, the chance for many to do *relatively* well materially was real in America, as was the probability of an absolute rising standard of living. It continued, if with difficulty and government contributions, as manufacturing and commerce transformed the nation in the mid-1800s, making it far more productive, with good jobs in cities and factories, stores and sales, and in the clerical offices of growing giant companies, all replacing the farming life. The twentieth century thus saw the development of a consumer society and a middle class, with considerable help from government. Constant if cyclical economic progress bore deeply into American thinking.

It is disturbing to see how many economists are unaware of such history, which is why I reemphasized it above. Even more inexplicably, they eschew the view that American workers have not fared well in the past thirty years. Even when incomes stagnate, or rise at best slowly, some find reasons to claim that workers are doing much better than they once did and that those who say otherwise choose to overstate the case. Life spans are somewhat longer than they were thirty years ago, and medical care is improved. The latter point is a favorite of some economists, who argue that the extension of life span is so valuable as to change radically our notion of the size of GDP.[31]

But life spans were extended far more dramatically early in the twentieth century due to improved public sanitation and water supplies, the minimization of small pox, cholera and other serious life threatening diseases, usually due to government programs, and by mid-century due to the advent of antibiotics and the polio vaccine, the latter administered by government. Yet, in addition to all that, real incomes earned on the job also rose robustly in those years.

Infant mortality is also down in recent years, we are reminded, if still significantly higher than in other rich nations. Airline fares are cheaper. Cars last longer (but they also cost much more).[32] More Americans own houses and those houses are marginally bigger (many observers cite the increase in the average rather than median size of the house, but the latter is up a mere 8 percent or so in twenty-five years, the equivalent of about a twelve by twelve foot room). Everyday clothes, tote bags, and even baseballs are often cheaper than they used to be, largely due to international trade.

The improved quality of many new products, some argued, meant inflation was overstated. If stated properly, real incomes rose more rapidly, and influential economists got the federal government to restate the data. But many agree the restatement may have been overdone. Yet some economists want more. Of course, if historical incomes had been restated, according to the criteria some economists now maintain is appropriate to adjust for quality gains like the extension of life and new products, income gains would have been implausibly high between the mid-1800s and the mid-1900s. Many of the current changes to data are also implausible.[33]

I have tried to make sense of why denial is so widespread. Republicans and the Right in general would understandably want to claim the economy has performed better than the conventional data show to justify the rise of laissez-faire econom-

ics since the 1980s. More troubling, many mainstream economists, liberal and conservative, may also want to overstate the
gains of the economy because they are dedicated to neoclassical economic policies, which have dominated thinking and
practice for three decades and in the process have tended to
minimize the importance of government. This includes a
painful policy focus on reducing inflation in particular. Inflation was surely tamed from its double-digit levels in the 1970s,
and it would be pleasant to believe the standard of living rose
handsomely in response, but for all the success of low inflation,
the standard of living did not rise inexorably.

But why did Democrats and some on the Left also persist in
arguing that the economy performed better? First, of course,
the Clinton Administration chose to put the most favorable
light on its achievements. In fact, incomes rose rapidly in the
second half of the 1990s, and they rose equally as well—they
even rose somewhat faster for lower-income Americans than
higher-income Americans. Much of the economic expansion
was attributable, as noted, to overspeculation in the stock
market and an insupportable boom in housing prices, which
sustained high levels of borrowing. Nevertheless, the rise in incomes then did not adequately compensate for the stagnation
and decline of the preceding twenty to twenty-five years. Second, however, I think centrist Democrats, pragmatic about
winning elections, simply assessed and then parroted what the
constituency wanted to hear. Voters were not yet ready, they
believed, to comprehend the need for large-scale government
change, so the advice was to avoid alienating them. They had
been convinced that government was generally the cause of
their economic frustration since the inflationary and confus-
ing 1970s, the great propaganda victory of Republicans in the
1970s. These Democrats were not about to undertake reedu-
cating the constituency. They rather spin their own analysis a

different way instead of following the course a more objective analysis would dictate.

Here's a summary. The costs of health care, drugs, and education have risen much more than family incomes in the past few decades. Families now work longer hours—about two and a half or three months a year more of work on average. They often live farther from work, thus spending more time commuting. Kids must take longer to finish college, and borrow much more to pay their way. Two-worker families have new expenses that are rarely included in the data, such as a *good* second car, baby-sitters, take-out food, and cleaning help. Good full-time infant care can cost $2,000 per month in major urban areas. People have to move to expensive neighborhoods because the schools are better, and they take on large mortgages. Debt is way up as a result, and we saw the devastating results in late 2007 and early 2008 as the subprime crisis spread to the rest of the credit-creating community. Bankruptcies are also up, as noted. Lay-offs are up. And on and on. The wide availability of debt and the rise in spousal work delayed recognition of the weaknesses in the economy.[34]

Are we now jeopardizing the equality of opportunity because people cannot afford the tools provided by good education, good health care and, a point to be raised later, good access to jobs and careers? Is the broad, positive definition of freedom, as discussed by Wilson, Roosevelt, and Johnson, and I would argue Jefferson and Lincoln, under assault? In the process, are individual rights under assault as well?

I would say yes. The deniers of the shift in economic benefits do the nation a serious disservice. In summary, they habitually ignore several important issues. When the median stagnates, as we've noted, it means a large proportion of workers, even if not a majority, fall behind. If one third of adults measurably see their real incomes reduced over a generation, compared to one sixth in the past, how bad is that, especially when most of the rest have very modest gains? What proportion of such adults is necessary to cause general dissatisfaction in the electorate? It need not be a majority. Combine the numbers of those who literally fall behind with those who make only slight progress (and must, judging by historical standards, be frustrated by their small gains), and they form a large majority. Some argue that women have done relatively well. In truth their gains have not been significant over time, and they still, as noted, typically make significantly less than do men with similar educations. Nor is the claim that women are doing better a comfort to men whose incomes are stagnating. The men must cope with the ahistorical flattening out of earnings that is neither explained to them nor well understood by them.

Also, stagnation is not only about jobs, wages, and salaries. Stagnating incomes around the median also imply that business opportunities are fewer than in normal historical periods. Many new businesses were started in the generation we are discussing, but there was a very high rate of failure and bankruptcy.

Let me also reemphasize that even if incomes discounted for inflation rise somewhat, this is a remarkably poor showing historically. Incomes rose more rapidly in the past, when such absolute economic mobility characterized America. Americans had long expected better than marginal increases in real income every thirty years; they had always achieved it. But even more important, if a bit subtle, rapidly rising incomes are not necessary for Americans to buy some items, such as more food and clothing, and even a higher quality and choice of both. But the rising costs of other items, often less tangible ones, are out of reach if incomes grow at historically modest rates. It happens that some of these items are critical: education, health care, drugs, and child care. The cost of public transportation has risen much more rapidly than other costs.

Prohibitive cost is the principal reason more than forty-five million Americans have no health insurance, many of whom are from families where at least one worker has a full-time job. When the Bureau of Labor Statistics discounts our actual incomes for rising prices, it bases the adjustment on a package of goods and services that is representative of actual purchases. This package is updated over time, and some economists argue that the current package already reflects a higher standard of living than the former package. This may require a brief explanation. A worker who earns the same amount of real wages can theoretically buy the same amount of the new package as he or she could once buy of the old package. There are usually fewer necessities in the new package because people earn nominally more and the costs of, for example, milk or shirts may have risen more slowly than typical incomes, leaving more income for other uses, even luxuries.

But this does not mean that if real incomes remain about the same, people are better off on balance because they can buy a few more so-called luxuries. In fact, they can buy fewer of other critical items. The key problem with this reasoning is that the needs of society change. What does it take to be middle class in America today? What may seem like a luxury becomes a necessity. Does anyone today think a telephone is a luxury? Based on the thinking of some economists, however, it should be thought of as one. Similarly, are cars truly luxuries as they once were? Some thought high school and surely college were luxuries in the past. More schooling is now a necessity. Day care, baby-sitters and take-out food are needed for the working spouse. Personal computers are not luxuries but necessities as the Internet expands its reach. A modern package of goods may seem superior to the older package in retrospect, but in the context of the times it likely is necessary just to tread water. It does not enable families to be more secure or provide a sense of progress.

In fact, in important respects this package is probably inferior because it reflects what people actually buy, and if prices go up for some goods and services they will usually buy fewer of them, not because they do not want or need them but because they are costly. In terms of the costs of health care and education, median wages and median family incomes have fallen well behind. People may more easily afford many kinds of food, and a wider variety of clothing, not to mention more electronics products (which make up a small percentage of consumer purchases, by the way), but affording health care is essentially impossible for a middle-class family, even of reduced size, unless one of the working members has a good job with adequate health care benefits. It is easier to buy yet another pair of shoes than dedicate one's budget to health care. And the coverage even for these jobs is falling. Meanwhile, getting a college education requires more borrowing, and family contributions. Even getting adequate K–12 education often requires buying into an expensive neighborhood, as noted. To make some sense of these numbers, we have to compare costs before inflation adjustments—actual dollars. In doing so, we find that the cost of health insurance has risen by four times since 1970, according to the federal government calculations, but median family income before inflation has only risen two and a half times. College costs have risen three times, drug costs by five times, and public transit by four times—all well more than nominal incomes. Discounting by inflation, based on a typical package of goods and services, simply does not capture this disadvantage. Another way of looking at this is to see how much faster education or health care costs have risen compared to all prices. According to the Bureau of Labor

Statistics (BLS), for example, the Consumer Price Index (CPI) is about twice what it was in the early 1980s, but the cost of tuition at private K–12 institutions has risen by five times and the cost of education books and supplies has risen by nearly four times. The cost of medical services and the cost of drugs have risen about three and a half times compared to the doubling of all prices.[35]

It's Not Just Inequality

What is particularly disturbing is that college has not been an adequate protection from slow economic growth for the male worker in the past thirty years. The gap between the pay of those with and without college started rising rapidly for both men and women in the late 1970s. Now, on average, a college graduate makes 40 to 45 percent more than a high school graduate. Over a lifetime, those with a college degree or higher will make twice what those with a high school degree will make.[36] Given such financial incentives, a higher proportion of Americans has gone to college. About 26 percent of all Americans over twenty-five have a bachelor's or more today, compared to 14 percent in 1975. About 40 percent of all those between twenty-five and thirty-four have a college degree or higher. Those with some college, a full four-year degree or a graduate degree, increased from roughly 35 percent of those employed to 56 percent.[37] But these levels have since been stagnating. If this seemed like success, however, it was mitigated by the modest growth in incomes for men with a college education. Moreover, going to college cost money in terms of tuition and time lost while in school. But the bifurcation in incomes between those who went to college and those who did not nevertheless became stark.

TABLE 6

Average Hourly Wage of Men (2005 dollars)

	High school	College	Advanced degree
1973	$17.41	$24.01	$26.67
2000	$15.74	$27.64	$34.54
2003	$15.65	$28.06	$35.67

Source: Mishel et al., *The State of Working America 2006/2007*, p. 151.

We can separate all male workers into those who received only a high school degree, those who finished schooling at a four-year college, and those who had graduate schooling. The hourly wage, after inflation, of men with a high school diploma fell from $17.41 in 1973 to $15.65 in 2005. These are averages, not median numbers, which would have shown a still steeper slide. By comparison, the average wage had roughly doubled in the twenty-five years up to 1973 for high school grads. Even those men with some college saw a decline in the average wage, if slight, since 1973. To earn a higher wage or salary, an average male needed a college degree. Even then, the average hourly wage rose only from $24.01 in 1973 to $28.06 in 2005, a little more than 15 percent over nearly thirty years. At least it was progress, but the increase was meager by former gains. Only those with an advanced degree did well, the real hourly wage rising from $26.67 in 1973 to $35.67 in 2005.[38]

If we look at median wages, we see that the typical male college graduate improved his hourly wage by only 12.8 percent since 1973. As noted, over more than thirty years, this is a trivial gain. College for the typical man was not a way to assure a middle-class life, when considering the rise in the costs of health care, education, and other products. For those near the lower end of the income distribution, college men actually lost ground over these years. But at least they did better than those

TABLE 7
Median Hourly Wage of Men

	High School	College
1973	$16.03	$20.61
2005	$13.82	$23.24

Source: Mishel et al., *The State of Working America
2006/2007*, p. 160.

with only high school degrees. The typical male high school
graduate saw real wages fall by about 15 percent over these
years.

Let's look further at college men. This may be the most dis-
heartening set of data. Median wages or salaries even for men
with college degrees did poorly over this period. Nikolaos Pa-
panikolaos and I looked at the annual incomes of full-time
male workers by age group. For unusually long periods of time,
the typical college worker made no gain at all. The median
young worker in the age group twenty-five to thirty-four experienced almost no rise since 1969. Those thirty-five to forty-
four experienced no gain from 1969 and 1989. Those in the
oldest age category, forty-five to fifty-four, had no gain since
1979. Within the group, there was rising inequality, however.
Some with college educations did well, others did not. But
college in itself was not the automatic answer to creating a
path to a middle-class life.[39]

Inequality is widely discussed in America today, but it can
misdirect our attention. Over this period, as we well know,
some Americans made a lot of money. One measure of this is
the prices paid for valuable art, which soared in the auctions of
2006. One painting by Willem de Kooning sold for nearly
$150 million in the fall of 2006. The growing inequality in an-
nual incomes rose to morally disturbing heights. It also raised

TABLE 8
Male Median Wage and Salary Income of Full-time, Year-round Workers by
Age and Educational Attainment, 1969–2005 (2005 dollars)

| Year | College (Four years/degree) | | |
	25–34	35–44	45–54
1969	$45,634	$54,760	$52,479
1979	$40,489	$54,816	$64,783
1989	$44,925	$54,731	$66,105
2000	$45,342	$58,945	$63,480
2005	$47,000	$63,000	$64,000

Source: Jeff Madrick and Nikolaos Papanikolaou analysis of United States Census
Bureau CPS data.

Note: Personal median wage and salary income is calculated for full-time workers,
35-plus hours per week, 50-plus weeks per year using CPI-U-RS index.

warning flags about the rise of monopoly economic power, on
Wall Street and elsewhere, that suggested at the least oligopo-
listic inefficiencies and perhaps manipulation, which contributed to the credit crisis of 2007 and 2008. When CEOs earn
some three-hundred times on average what the average worker
earns compared to thirty times in 1969, it merits concern.
When those men in the ninety-fifth percentile (only 5 percent
make more) earn three times what those in the middle of the
pack do compared to only two times thirty years earlier, the
fairness of the economy can be justifiably questioned.[40]

Many observers in these rationalizing times justify unequal
rewards for work both as the rising price of talent and as a
stimulus to others to work harder. But if the work of some is
being unjustly rewarded, as it almost surely is, an American
principle is uprooted. The erosion of faith in American fairness
is a tragic consequence of inequality. Are the unequal rewards
justified by the contribution of those who earn so much? Cred-

ible research shows this is not remotely true for top executives, for example.[41] Their rewards have increased much faster
than profits. If effort is rewarded unfairly, a good mainstream
economist would also argue that incentives are distorting investment and effort, channeling it inefficiently to where it is
wasted. Financial scandal in recent years, whose sheer ubiq-
uity has been breathtaking, also distorts the incentives of the
economy. Thus, unjustifiable inequality is corrosive of our faith
and our economy, and has had measurable psychological and
physical consequences.[42]

But to the extent that inequality became the short-hand
word to describe the lagging standard of living for so many
Americans, it diverted focus from underlying issues having to
do with the inadequacy of most wages and salaries. Stagnant
and falling wages for most Americans are greater concerns,
and they cannot be completely explained by rising income at
the top. If the total sum of wages and salaries had been distributed more along the lines of what they were in the 1960s,
American workers would still not have fared very well since
the 1970s because the economy itself did not grow rapidly
until the late 1990s. The principal reason then was the much
slower growth of productivity, or output of GDP per hour of
work, between the early 1970s and the mid-1990s. Also,
women worked in greater numbers and men seemed to be increasingly competing for a slower growing pot of earnings. In
economic terms, this was a long period of time.

Productivity, to repeat, is the key to economic growth and
a rising standard of living. If the GDP per working hour does
not increase, there will be no additional money with which to
pay workers an increase. We can't pay people more wages and
salaries over time if the output for the time put in does not
grow.

The standard of living started growing slowly since the early

1970s, because productivity began to grow slowly—to the surprise, it is fair to say, of every professional economist. In the 1970s, compensation at least kept up with productivity growth, but the relationship between the median standard of living and productivity growth started to break down, and then it came completely unhinged in the early 2000s. As *The State of Working America 2006–2007* shows, productivity grew by about 33 percent between 1995 and 2005, but compensation grew half that. Moreover, almost all the poor performance occurred in the early 2000s. The gap between productivity growth and wages grew to disturbing heights in the early 2000s.[43] Its causes are not clear, but a basic tenet of mainstream economics was challenged. If it were simply a function of the offshoring of work, the gap should not have started to widen in the 1980s. The degree of offshoring in the 2000s also did not expand as rapidly as did the gap between productivity and worker compensation. Some of the disconnect between wages and productivity may also be computational. Productivity gains may exaggerate the progress of the economy for technical reasons, such as the more rapid obsolescence of computer-oriented technology.[44] Whatever the causes, the implications are disturbing and represent a marked change in the very nature of economic growth and the distribution of its benefits that the nation cannot ignore.

■ ■ ■ ■ ■

Wages and salaries were not by any means the only disappointments of this period. Fairly early in the twentieth century, America as a nation by and large decided that private enterprise would provide it health insurance, not government. In the early decades of the post–World War II era, health insurance coverage expanded, and in 1965 the federal government provided Medicare for the elderly and Medicaid for the poor.

But, as mentioned, the private sector coverage began to decline in recent decades. In 2004, business provided health care coverage for approximately 56 percent of working Americans compared to 69 percent in 1979. Private pension coverage also fell, from slightly more than 50 percent in 2004 to 45.5 percent in 2004. The coverage for male workers alone fell far more drastically. In the case of health care coverage, it is down nearly 17 percentage points from 75.5 percent in 1979 to 58.5 percent in 2004. If we examine the data according to education, we also see especially radical reductions in coverage for those with a high school education. Business health insurance coverage for recent high school graduates fell from about 65 percent in the late 1970s to less than 40 percent in 2004. Pension coverage also fell for new high school graduates in the job market. For recent college graduates, coverage has fallen but not nearly as significantly.[45]

Such disadvantages for high school graduates further suggest a new class bias in the American economy. The labor market is decidedly working against these Americans. So is the path to college. It is blocked by socioeconomic background. Even when teenagers from poorer families do well on college entrance exams, they are less likely to complete college than better-off teenagers with the same scores. A far higher proportion of youth from high-income families attend the best schools; those from lower incomes disproportionately attend community colleges.[46] As one college president has put it, tell me what college you are in and I'll tell you what zip code you are from.[47]

Another concern is the lack of progress in closing racial gaps in wages and overall compensation. Black families by and large earn 60 percent of what white families earn. This has changed little over thirty years. Women, despite rising earnings, make about 80 percent of what men do, and even with comparable educations make only 90 percent of what men do. An economy working supposedly according to neoclassical principles should not produce such gaps. For racial discrimination, one study was particular stunning. Researchers sent identical resumes to a business, but changed the names to suggest that some of the applicants were African Americans. The difference in response to the same resumes with changed names was remarkable, some three and a half decades after the Great Society programs were passed. [48]

I end this section with one last argument. Those who believe that someone earning $60,000 a year in 2005, for example, is roughly doing as well as someone who earned $60,000 in 1979, adjusting those 1979 dollars for inflation, understates not merely the increase in the costs of education, health care and so on, but also a sharp rise in the anxiety of American life. American life has gotten riskier for most workers. Now, it is at last becoming clear that jobs are less secure, and they are of shorter duration.[49] Less secure jobs means less secure health insurance and pensions benefits. Because children require good educations that often mean living in expensive neighborhoods, threats to the family income are now threats to one's children's future. In the past, the differentiation among such schools and neighborhoods, though evident, was less important because a broad cross section of America got adequate and secure jobs no matter where they went to college. In the past, a parent could afford to stay home and nourish the family. The median family works about thirteen weeks more a year than it once did, most of it the extra hours now worked by the spouse. These are new sources of anxiety for workers that comparisons of real incomes do not reflect.[50] Women should of course not be asked to stay home, they should be helped to make work more productive and less anxious and costly, otherwise they remained discriminated against. It is simply a

new form of discrimination. Thus, comparing incomes today
to those in the past neglects addressing the pressures of life
due to the new insecurities. In the past, quite the opposite was
occurring. Insecurities were being reduced by rising benefits
and greater job security, even as real wages and salaries were
rising rapidly.

When Knowledge Also Changes

I have focused on the poor economic performance since the
1970s in part because the severity of the changes is underem-
phasized in the political discourse about what ails the nation.
America was always a nation whose identity and political
attitudes were closely aligned with the material gain of its
citizens. Such material gain, beginning with the ownership
of property, not only conferred personal freedom from life-
threatening wants but also conferred status and self-esteem. It
not only conferred self-esteem but also political independence. It also, finally, conferred a sense of personal or psychological security, a place in the world that was more certain.

The sense of security was perhaps the most remarkable
achievement of all. The poor performance of the economy and
a stagnating or falling standard of living for so many Americans
since the 1970s has undermined all these. That retirement security and health care are dependent on a job in America adds
to the anxiety, which is not the case in many other rich nations.
The fear of losing a job is thus compounded by the loss of
health insurance and pensions. In turn, inequality, which has
left many working and poor Americans out of the pool of
people to benefit fully from advanced medicine, good teach-
ing, communications, and social networks, is insidious as well

because of the damage to self-esteem. We have backtracked seriously on the traditional promises of what America can offer.

At least until very recently we have almost purposefully refused to believe in the nation's deteriorating economic prospects; and we neglect managing change as a purpose of government. But having said that, economic prospects are not all that have changed. What has also changed, and what constantly changes, is what we as a society know.

I will now discuss a few critical areas in which I think our knowledge has clearly improved. This, as I have stated, is also a form of change with which we must deal. We know almost unambiguously a lot more about the intellectual and social development of children. There is considerable evidence that emotional and intellectual nourishment, as well as adequate food and medical care in the early years of life, are critical to leading full and productive lives.

Moreover, these programs can produce financial returns to the community due to fewer children in special education programs, reduced crime, fewer of these children joining future welfare roles as adults, and the freeing of parental time to work.[51] One study claims that if similar educational benefits were supplied to all three- and four-year-olds in poverty, the financial benefits to society would equal nine times the costs.[52] Even if such cost-benefit analyses significantly overstate the benefits, the implications are still powerful. Early education, improved day care, and reduction in the poverty of adult parents can have enormous pay-offs for the children involved and society in general.

We know that an emphasis on preventive care such as exercise, diet, and early diagnosis of diseases can profoundly improve health outcomes and reduce costs. We now have drugs that can reduce the likelihood of heart attacks, but far too few of those at risk take them. We know that if arthritis is treated early, it can prevent future disabilities. We know that hundreds of thousands of children with asthma do not see doctors, who have the tools to ease their lives. We increasingly know that there are psychological components to disease, and that some psychological disturbances are treatable diseases as well.[53] Depression is an example, as is attention deficit disorder. We now know that learning disabilities, such as dyslexia, are every bit as damaging as are physical disabilities, and we have learned more about how to mainstream young Americans who are so afflicted.

Among the most conspicuous advances in knowledge are medical breakthroughs, notably in the control of coronary disease but in other areas as well, such as prosthetics. Our expectations for a longer and better life have therefore risen with these innovations. Do we not have a responsibility to make these as widely available as possible, like we once made small pox or polio vaccines available, or the way we make special education available to those with learning disabilities?

In other spheres of life, there is no longer a stigma attached to a wife working. This is a major and especially welcome change from the 1950s. Divorce is also generally accepted, meaning that a single woman is more free socially to remain so, as are single mothers. Single-parent families are ever more common, and, increasingly, out-of-wedlock children are socially acceptable.

The nation has seriously broadened its views of acceptable behavior in other ways. African Americans now routinely appear as leading men and women in our movies and TV programs. Not long ago, it was a taboo for a whites and blacks to kiss on screen. And there are, as has been brought home in the 2008 presidential race, many more "mixed" marriages in America. Similarly, there are countless programs about gays and lesbians. Of course, there is also a vociferous and strongly felt backlash to these changes. There has also been a restructuring of religious participation across the nation, with a decided rise in evangelical Christians and a corresponding loss for more mainstream protestant religions.[54] Yet we should also remember that, if much of the evangelical movement rejects change or seeks to turn back to an imaginary past, there is also evident a wave of progressive evangelicism that seeks to deal with change and new knowledge.

We know much more about the impact of industrialization on the environment and the planet's resources. There are still unknowns about the likely course of global warming, for example, but they are fewer than they once were. Warnings about the availability of natural resources have for two hundreds years been proved wrong, but such resources are becoming much more expensive to develop.

All these issues contribute to radically changed expectations about a decent life. They challenge older notions about what it means to have equal opportunity. If a decent pre-K education is critical to success and future equality of opportunity, is a public education system which starts with kindergarten adequate? Can a society tolerate an unequal public school system, in which poorer Americans systematically receive inferior services? If college is now a necessity, as high school once was, should government make it free? At the other end of the age spectrum, if we work later in life, should we be entitled to job training throughout life? In terms of health, if drugs and treatments are widely known to work, at what point do we stop requiring people to pay for them? When does a historical luxury become a contemporary right? If a decent environment is vital to a full life, how much is a society willing to pay for it? Can it be decided in the marketplace or must it be decided collectively?

There are also the new high technology products of the age.

Today, a PC and access to the Internet are requirements for a decent life. We communicate with it, we learn from the Internet, we need it for schooling, and we work with it. How disadvantaged are those who cannot afford a PC? American public schools generally once supplied free textbooks to its students. Should they provide PCs and Internet service to access the information needed for today's living?

Entertainment has been revolutionized by new products. Here free markets seem to work well. We are not obliged to be sure everyone has an iPod or a cell phone. New technologies simply have winners and losers. It is a lot cheaper to rent a DVD than to go to the neighborhood movie house, thus making such entertainment more accessible to the poor. As has been widely discussed, American youngsters can learn by playing video games. But we should also understand that when cheap telephone booths are removed across America, those who don't have cell phones are put at a disadvantage. As once-free TV coverage of baseball games are moved to cable, those who don't have cable are disadvantaged. And those who don't have a PC are indeed at a disadvantage in simply being informed and educated. These represent new inequalities. They are not simply deprivations from luxuries; such products are increasingly necessities.

The Purpose of Government

The most radical shifts in American life are clear. At the heart of it is poor wage growth and the rapidly rising cost of key services like health care and education. This has generated profound changes in the nation's social structure. Among families, two-worker families are the largest category. Most Americans now go to college for some period of time, but increasingly people recognize that some form of education should start as early as possible. Health care is very expensive compared to incomes and may soon reach 20 percent or more of GDP—far higher than what we pay today, which is already far higher than any other country pays. In general, economic life is less secure—as jobs are less secure, so are the health care and pension benefits attached to them.

Adding deeply to the insecurity is the high level of debt. American's total borrowing has risen rapidly, especially in the 2000s. There was once fifty cents of household debt for every dollar of annual consumer income. Now there is $1.20 of household debt for every dollar of income. Rising debt leaves Americans more vulnerable to lost jobs, rising interest rates and, as in 2007 and 2008, sudden falls in the value of assets, notably houses and stocks. High levels of debt have meant that when the housing market turned down many lost their homes. Debt and lost home equity also jeopardize retirement incomes.[55]

There are at least two major categories of rising international threats to America. The first includes the threat of terrorism, growing instability in the world, and devastating weaponry, which have raised costs and risks for all Americans. The second is the globalization of trade and capital, America's dependence on foreign investment, and the rapid rise of new economic powers. A few years ago, naïve and ideological scholars heralded the rise of a benevolent American hegemony as the world's sole superpower. Today, we know that such power is severely limited. So entwined are the world's economies that no single economy is autonomous. An interlocking capitalist world may well require new forms of generally agreed upon regulation and control that sometimes violate the best interests of the United States.

It is highly unlikely America will dominate the world economy in fifty years. To someone born in the late 1940s, like myself, fifty years has become a short period of time. America's ability to borrow in such great quantity has been dependent on its dominance in the world markets and the role of the dollar as the leading currency of the age. This central fact will change. Thus, foreign and domestic policy, which for its entire history the nation was able to separate, will no longer be disconnected.

Meantime, the costs of investing in ourselves in order to maintain a middle-class life have increased significantly. In particular, we all require more education. But health care is also far more expensive—our most significant future cost. There is also the high cost of neglect. For a generation, the nation has neglected addressing change. Thus, our health care system awaits true crisis to be adequately fixed, there is no pre-K education widely available, the safety net in an age of rapid technological change and rising international competition is inadequate, public investment in transportation has been cut, while infrastructure gets an average grade of D from the experts. The quality of education has become a function of the class into which one is born. The financial community has been allowed and even encouraged through reduced and lax regulation to run amok with other people's money.

Finally, and in summary, have we come to a time when Americans can no longer expect a rising standard of living? Globalization is a contributor but not the explanation. As noted, the world has been globalizing rapidly since World War II. Is there little that can be done? How then do we address change?

Forsaking Pragmatism for Ideology

We do not know all the causes of the economic and social changes of the past three decades. We do know many of the consequences. We also know that those consequences in turn have consequences. The largest mystery remains, as it always had, why productivity grows, or fails to do so. Essentially, Adam Smith wrote *The Wealth of Nations* to answer the question of why wealth had begun to rise rapidly in Great Britain in the 1700s; it was the early stages of the industrial revolution. Few economists would claim they know why productivity growth slowed down beginning in 1973; no economist, quite literally, predicted this in the 1960s or even the 1970s, when the trend was already underway. Even if we understood the causes, we might not have remedies.

But after more than two hundred years of thinking about the subject and testing hypotheses, economists do know some things about why economies grow. The problem is when we reduce the determinants to a standard few, to make rather grandiose claims about them, and to infuse the analysis with an ideology about free markets. Education, transportation, and institutions that support markets—such as private contracts, private property, and stable national finances—certainly matter, for example. In my view, the size of domestic markets or trade union markets make a substantial contribution; current mainstream theory incorrectly neglects this. Scientific and technological advance are critical to growth and provide benefits best when access to them is less restricted by copyright or patent. Economists know that a variety of forms of capitalism have produced similar rates of growth: the Nordic welfare states, for example, do not take a back seat in results to the American model of limited government. It is proof of the ambiguity of growth theory. Thus, as we have taken pains to make clear in Part I, arguments about the size and extent of government are often simplistic; the question is rather, what government does and how well it does it. On the other hand, we do know, without embracing ideological points of view, that centralized planning, as practiced in the Soviet Union, has serious practical limits the most important of which is the suppression of information about what consumers and business need and want. I believe that large markets and democratic aims both critically contributed to growth, subjects too often neglected in neoclassical economics.

We do know slow growth since 1973 has had serious consequences. Slow productivity growth in itself tells us little about why male wages stagnated while female wages rose, or why the racial gap in wages remains. Again, it is not sweeping generalizations but the particulars that matter. We do know that the rise of the two-worker family, the major social transformation of the era, was partly the consequence of stagnant male wages, but also partly the consequence of a vibrant social recognition of the needs, desires, and rights of women. Do we deal with the causes of change or the consequences? We should deal with what we know or can make solid, educated deductions about, and this is the course we will take in the next section of the book.

But the constructive adjustment to change requires active, innovative, and bold government. A nation, first of all, should recognize it must deal with change if it is to survive, evolve, prosper, and maintain its ideals. It should deal in particular with those changes in social and economic conditions and knowledge that newly challenge its deepest values—in America's case, I believe they are freedom and equality. In modern times, such political values cannot readily be separated from prosperity, as we shall see. But America is not dealing with what is standing before it, in part because it has retreated into a misplaced nostalgia for a role of government that never really existed. This reflects fear not optimism.

In the past thirty-five years, America has been in thrall to laissez-faire government, but after a generation it is time to take stock. The promises made by the laissez-faire advocates have not been kept. The nation has not solved most of its major problems. It remains rich and retains its enormous entrepreneurial energy. But we are not even sure rapid productivity growth has returned permanently. What we do know is that in the past five years productivity has grown while wages and family incomes have largely stagnated, after having done so for more than twenty years between 1973 and 1995. We do know that individual Americans and business borrow prodigiously and at rates that are probably not sustainable. We do know that basic sources of growth, such as education and transportation, have not been adequately improved. We do know that costs for the middle class have risen far more rapidly than incomes— health care and education, in particular. We know that child poverty remains intractable and that the nation's health care does not provide the results that it pays for. We know the nation has the highest incarceration rates in the rich world. We know transportation infrastructure is either decaying or falling behind world standards.

Thus, we know that the popular political and economic views of the past thirty years have failed in many respects. In my view, they have failed because pragmatic solutions have been forsaken for ideology; these solutions have been based on a narrow, backward-looking view of the purpose of government. Change simply has not been adequately addressed in America. It requires government to do so. Part III presents a range of ideas about the problems to be addressed and what the nation can do.

PART III

....

WHAT TO DO

Pessimism in America

HOW DID America become a nation that does not believe it can afford to do what it once did and to do what has to be done today? How did the wealthiest nation in history come to believe it is not wealthy? Part of the nation's new agenda must be to rid itself of a deep-seated pessimism that it does not acknowledge. Ronald Reagan, promising a "new morning in America," ironically ushered in the age of limits he accused Jimmy Carter of creating. With Reagan, slow wage growth and high levels of unemployment became accepted. Pundits like Robert Samuelson of *Newsweek* and many like-minded observers told America that fast wage growth in the 1950s and 1960s was an aberration in its history, and they should be satisfied with the slow progress and even broad declines of average wages in the 1970s and 1980s, given how far the nation had already come.[1] New institutions to cope with the rising two-worker family were never seriously considered; Americans simply worked more. People were told not that they would be helped to lead fuller lives but, as both Republican and moderate Democratic experts claimed, that they should be well-satisfied. Had the Reagan spirit of government distrust prevailed throughout American history, property in America would probably not have been distributed as equitably as it was in the early years, the free primary and high schools of America would probably not have been built, the highways would have been an uncoordinated and inadequate maze, minorities would not have been as readily included in the economy, and GIs would not have been subsidized to go to college.

The free market ideologues have told us all this would have happened, anyway—and more efficiently. But look what has happened to America in the last thirty-five years—when this ideology was ascendant.

Today, in an age of limits of which the nation's policymakers seem quite proud, including Clintonian Democrats, America has no free and high-quality day care or pre-K institutions to nourish and comfort two-worker families, and both work and family are undermined as consequence. College has become far more expensive and attendance is now bifurcated by class: the privileged now go to the best colleges, and good jobs are increasingly available only to those who attend the best colleges. Transportation infrastructure has been notoriously neglected, is decaying, and has not been adequately modernized to meet energy-efficient standards or global competition. America has not responded to a new world of high energy costs and global warming in general. America has a health care system that is simply out of control, providing on balance inadequate quality at very high prices—specializing in high-technology medicine at the expense of better overall care. The financial system, progressively deregulated since the 1970s, broke free of government oversight entirely in the 1990s and early 2000s and speculation reminiscent of the 1800s was the result, with potentially equal levels of damage. And, of course, average incomes have been flat to only slightly higher; for men, that has been true since the early 1970s. These facts amount to about as conclusive a proof as history ever provides that the ideology applied in this generation has failed.

Under the influence of this ideology and mythological "looking back" narratives, many Americans still reflexively see government as an intrusive force, and are unaware or deliberately forgetful of its many past accomplishments. They see their own more difficult lives as inevitable, and if strained, it is the case because of social programs adopted by government, not the consequence of government's failure to act. A life of family strain, inequality, and insecurity has become accepted as inevitable. It is even thought to be a strength of America. This was Reagan's Trojan horse, disguised as optimism.[2] Your suffering was the result of government, but to improve our conditions we should suffer some more. He sent in a plan to reduce help to most Americans under the guise of an ideology of personal responsibility that would ultimately make everyone better off, but instead largely helped an increasingly privileged upper tier.

The absurd levels of remuneration on Wall Street are the leading example of a nation divorced from reality by ideology. They are the result, we were told by some policymakers and serious scholars, of a natural process of the free market in a modern economy, justified by the alleged contributions Wall Street professionals make to the economy. The following real problems apparently do not change the collective mind: a savings and loan scandal that cost hundreds of billions of dollars; a stock market crash in 1987; an international financial debacle in 1997 and 1998; corporate scandals led by Enron in which employees lost life savings in the early 2000s; and a deep credit crisis due to insupportable prices for houses in 2007 and 2008—all undergirded by an extraordinary shift of the annual national income to the top 1 percent of earners. Perhaps as I write this, the current crisis will bring about more serious change. As we go to press, the people are choosing a new president and the opinion surveys reflect a deep and palpable dissatisfaction with the economy. But the response may well be too late and is likely to be too little, and whatever reforms come may be poorly designed and administered.

In fact, enlightened regulation has been imperative for economic growth at least since Jefferson's policies for governing the distribution of land. When done well, regulation keeps competition honest and free, enables customers to know and understand the products they receive, and fosters new ideas. When neglected, abuse becomes easy, information in markets is suppressed, capital investment is channeled to wasteful and inefficient uses, and dangerous excesses occur. The open flow of products and services information is critical to a free-market economy. The conditions for healthy competition have simply not been maintained under a free-market ideology of minimal government that professes great faith in competition. Competition requires government oversight; the wool has been pulled over our eyes.

We now know the following. If federal, state, and local governments absorb roughly 35 percent of GDP in America, rather than the current roughly 30 percent, it will not inhibit growth and undermine entrepreneurial spirits, productivity, or prosperity if the spending is well-channeled. Government absorbs much more of national income in other nations whose prosperity is the equivalent of or perhaps superior to America's. In European nations, government spending absorbs approximately 40 percent of all spending, and standards of living are high. If government programs are managed well, they will on balance enhance productivity. A rise to 35 percent will raise approximately $700 billion a year to the federal, state, and local governments to provide protections to workers, finance social programs, maintain an adequate regulatory presence, and raise significantly the level of investment in transportation, energy, education, and health care. Part and perhaps all of this $700 billion can be paid for with higher taxes.

Let's try to keep the discussion more practical, however. If we lower our sights to a an additional and more politically practicable 3 percent of GDP for new government programs, the nation would have more than $400 billion a year with which to work. Four hundred billion dollars a year could make Social Security entirely solvent by current estimates, with no further reductions in benefits, provide universal pre-K education to America's three-to-five-year-olds, and leave fifty or sixty billion dollars to be shared with state and local government to improve education. Or we could set aside thirty to fifty billion dollars a year, which could fully pay for two years of tuition for all college students. Thirty billion dollars a year could also go a long way toward repairing and updating transportation infrastructure, and making it far more energy efficient. Some competent scientists argue we could transform the nation from fossil fuel to solar energy for only a little more than that a year.[3]

What seem to many in America like pragmatic limitations about spending, the proper role of government or responsible fiscal management will very likely someday be seen for what they truly are: a reflection of a deep pessimism, the rise in power of vested interests seeking tax cuts and special benefits, and a tragic foregoing of responsibility. Boldness of government does not mean that the right choices will always be made. The war in Iraq serves as a supreme and tragic reminder of government activism gone awry. And there are other errors, some of them made by liberals. It is hard to terminate government programs once started, for example. But we tolerate wrong choices and a lot of waste in business in order not to suppress its "animal spirits." And it is also hard to shut down businesses: consider the bailouts of Chrysler, Continental Illinois, and the government support of Bear Stearns most recently. Such examples understate the breadth of government bailouts. When the Federal Reserve rapidly loosened monetary policies in 1972, 1987, 1998, and 2001, much of the motivation was to bailout business.

We must encourage experimentation and boldness in government as well as in business. History emphatically tells us that the results can be constructive and, more to the point, tells us that unrestrained business is not enough to preserve prosperity and equal opportunity.

Part III of this book is about renewing faith that America has the resources and capabilities to recapture its energies and optimism. Despite so much antagonism to the idea, government can and must be a full partner to business in American economic development and a senior partner in the equitable distribution of benefits and true practical freedoms. What history and contemporary examples teach us is that the nation has the capacity to regulate, tax, and invest adequately in public goods without undermining the entrepreneurial capacity and material prosperity of the nation. The nation needs an understanding of its history; with understanding, I believe the will to act may follow. This section will offer a somewhat detailed agenda, but the spirit of its proposals is far more important than the details. Another set of proposals with different details may well work as well. I offer what follows only as a rough and practical guide to what is possible, not as a detailed, formal program.

The Failure of Conventional Wisdom

But first, let's identify the leading scapegoats thought responsible for our current ills, because too much attention paid them will not meet the nation's challenges. There is a bad habit among the free-market advocates and a variety of others to blame America's difficulties on consumers who do not save enough. By the mid-2000s, the national savings rate had actually turned negative. Overall, there was more spending than earning, in other words, and people borrowed to make up the difference. Because total savings were so low, the nation required funds from overseas to finance its investment, pushing the value of the dollar too high. The high dollar undermined American manufacturing exports and good manufacturing jobs. Meantime, Americans are now heavily indebted and less able to withstand a downturn.

But keep in mind how little earnings have risen for more than a full generation of workers. Are average Americans really on a buying spree? Can they merely be encouraged to save more? They are buying inexpensive imports from China and elsewhere at stores like Wal-Mart, mostly clothing, accessories, and minor furnishings. They are buying more electronics goods partly because prices have fallen so rapidly. But compare these to the rapid rise in the costs of essential services to a decent life: education, health care, housing, and the myriad costs of maintaining a two-worker family, including housekeeping, meals out, extra cars, gasoline for commuting, and so on. Americans must buy houses they probably can't afford to get their children into good school districts. College students take out much more than they once did in student loans to go to college. Americans increasingly lose health care coverage.

Did Americans really embark on a consumerist society? Cars are more affordable because of far lower interest rates, which reduce annual leasing costs. People borrowed against their homes to pay college tuitions. The proportion of those who own homes in America rose rapidly because people borrowed beyond their means, resulting in the 2008 sub-prime mortgage crisis. The persistently poor have not saved less in order to splurge, yet the rate of credit card borrowing among the relatively poor is high.

There has surely been some effort to keep up with the ever-richer Joneses in America. But the issue should be kept in perspective. Americans would have saved more had they earned more money. Thus, cajoling them to save more by giving them, for example, bigger tax breaks, has not worked. Investments in tax protected 401(k)s have soared but Americans have not saved more. One surer way to raise savings would be to raise wages.

Similarly, one of the main reasons to argue for a reduced budget deficit or even a surplus is to increase the nation's total savings. A deficit withdraws savings from the economy and vice versa. Despite the higher level of savings due to the surplus in the late 1990s, the U.S. dollar continued to climb and Americans imported foreign goods in greater volume. The trade deficit rose rapidly to levels that had all concerned. More savings in America did not squelch the imbalances that so many claimed it would; the trade deficit only grew.

In particular, inflation earned its place as the nation's main problem in the 1970s, and held its position until the present. The current Federal Reserve chairman, Ben Bernanke had argued strenuously as a professor at Princeton that maintaining low rates of inflation—so-called inflation targeting—was the path to economic stability and ideal rates of growth. The Federal Reserve under Alan Greenspan indeed achieved consistently low inflation. Yet over that period, there was intense speculation in stocks and housing that eventually led to crashes. There were also two enormous credit crises. The first was an international debacle in 1997 and 1998, eventually resulting in the demise of the huge hedge fund, Long-Term Capital Management. The second started in 2007 and is not completed as of this writing: the sub-prime mortgage crisis, which spread rapidly to other kinds of debt instruments.

Such a focus on inflation, then, is not an adequate safeguard for the economy. Nor is the focus on budget balancing. In the late 1990s, the nation did precisely what mainstream economists demanded by eliminating the budget deficit and keeping inflation low. But the conditions were set for a market and housing bust, a recession in 2001 and again in 2008, and the most dangerous credit conditions since the 1920s.

Moreover, the focus on low inflation may have contributed to the poor wage performance of recent decades. The Federal Reserve tended to step on the brakes—that is, raise rates— whenever wages rose faster than they favored. The inflation focus began in the 1970s. Paul Volcker, the Federal Reserve chairman appointed by Jimmy Carter in 1979, adopted a highly stringent policy in mid-1980 to break the back of double-digit inflation and high interest rates. It succeeded, but at the cost of severe recession in 1982 in the United States and complete disarray in many developing nations. Many believed his deter- mination and stringent policy were the nation's only choices. I have some doubts about this, but it became the overwhelming conventional wisdom.[4] From that point until the mid-1990s, unemployment rates were kept at historically high rates in the United States to forestall inflation. Wage increases were thought to be the main cause of higher prices as business raised prices to maintain profit margins. Wage increases remained subdued, and a low-wage economy became accepted, even praised.

Before the credit turmoil and rising energy prices, the in- formal inflation target was 2 to 2.5 percent a year. The nation had stability in growth rates, yet key imbalances remained: the large trade deficit, an insupportably high dollar, high levels of debt, and highly volatile financial markets. Some mainstream economists believe inflation can reach as high as 3 percent or more a year without jeopardizing ever rising prices and sig- nificantly higher interest rates.[5] If such a rate was the target, or at the least, the inflation target was flexible, real wages may have risen more rapidly. The economy would not be reigned in as quickly every time the inflation target was even moderately exceeded. Such arguments challenge conventional wisdom, clearly, but the conventional wisdom has partly been the result of the acceptance of an age of limits. It may now be changing.

Most disturbing, under the aegis of limitation and neglect, as discussed earlier, America increasingly has become a society in which birth determines one's future—a class society. Some research now suggests that as much as 60 percent of a person's income is correlated to one's father's income. This would mean that there is relatively little escape from one's upbringing. Twenty years ago, some economists claimed triumphantly, notably those with a conservative point of view, that only 20 percent of a person's income was determined by one's father's income, and reveled in the evidence that the American dream was alive and well because Americans had a high chance of rising above the station of their parents. It is not nearly 20 percent, however. Some economists believe the correlation is closer to 40 percent, but no one any longer believes it is below that.[6]

College attendance and completion, and in particular attendance at high quality colleges, are closely related to whether and where one's parents went to college, and generally on the socioeconomic status of the parents. Thus, once seen as a way out, the rising need for a college degree is reinforcing socioeconomic differences, not breaking them down. Those who don't start out well—through no fault of their own—remain where they are, in part because they don't go to good colleges.[7]

Business as usual will not work in coming decades. Conventional attitudes about inflation, savings, and budgets are often wrong or not adequate in addressing important issues. They reflect the general belief that conditions must merely be set to let the markets work, and to minimize government intrusion.[8] Is the nation truly as helpless before such questions as it seems? Will it again accept the same answer that failed it in the past?

■ ■ ■ ■ ■

The purpose of this book is to convey a sense of possibilities that a generation ago would not have been thought unwieldy or impossible to implement. I begin with raising money through taxes. Can America raise another $400 billion in taxes, a total of 3 percent or so of GDP? I will now simply make general and approximate suggestions to give a sense of some of the possible alternatives, should the nation choose to fully pay the costs of social programs—that in a contemporary light seem substantial but in the light of history are both necessary and workable.

Regarding tax revenues, let's start with a potential tax on wealth, which if common in a number of nations, has never earned a serious quorum of adherents in America. We can get a sense of the potential to raise money rather easily. The assets of the wealthy have increased disproportionately and rapidly in the last three decades. Wealth, or net worth, is customarily defined as the sum of the value of a house and all stocks, bonds, insurance policies, and other financial assets, less mortgage and consumer and other debt. It has risen on average two to three times faster than incomes since the 1970s, as equity values and house prices rose.[9] Falling interest rates in particular have raised the value of investments in bonds and stocks, as well as house prices. A reasonable estimate of the total value of all real estate and financial assets less debt of American households is roughly $40 trillion. The top 1 percent of Americans control roughly 35 percent of wealth in the nation, or more than $12 trillion. By comparison, they controlled only 20 percent or so in the early 1970s. The mean net worth of the top 20 percent has risen by roughly 75 percent since the early 1980s, and is now more than twenty times the average net worth of those in the middle fifth of the nation. In the early 1980s, it was fifteen times the net worth of the middle fifth.[10]

The top 5 percent of the wealthy have a net worth of $24 trillion, more than $4 million on average per person. The mean net worth of the top 20 percent of American households is nearly $2 million, in total some $32 trillion.

To the question of where the money is, the answer is in these assets. It is entirely reasonable to raise $150 billion annually without great penalty to the nation's wealthy. There can be many variations to arrive at the desired amount. Wealth taxes are levied in European nations such as Sweden, Switzerland, and Germany. They equal about 20 percent of income taxes. If the wealth tax was levied to equal about 20 percent of income taxes in America, it would yield roughly $200 billion a year.[11] If the wealth of the richest 20 percent of Americans were taxed at the rate of 0.5 percent a year, it would raise roughly $160 billion a year. The rate could be graduated as well, with lower rates for those with a smaller net worth, higher at the upper end.

But other sources of revenue are also available, which could supplement or be substituted in part for the wealth tax—and raise even more money. The high inequality of incomes in the nation suggests that taxes on high earners make sense. There is another strong argument, based on a wide range of recent studies, which suggests that high earners spend increasingly on positional goods that confer status. But this is typically a no-win game because as incomes rise one must spend more to stay in place.[12] It also has invidious consequences for those who cannot keep up.[13] If income tax rates—including the alternative minimum tax and rates paid on dividends and capital gains—were raised for all tax brackets by three percentage points or so, it would raise roughly $120 billion more in tax revenue. We could raise the lower tax brackets by less by raising the upper tax brackets by more, of course. Raising the top three brackets by another one percentage point would raise roughly $20 billion more, enabling reduction in rates for lower income individuals.[14]

Changes can also be made in the amount individuals can deduct from their taxable income such as home mortgage interest, state and local taxes, and medical expenses. Reasonable limitations on such deductions, which would usually affect better off Americans more than others, could raise $50 billion and more annually within a couple of years.[15]

Corporate taxes paid to the U.S. government have fallen over time 2 percent of GDP from about 3 percent in the 1970s and 4 and 5 percent in the 1950s and 1960s. This has been the result of reduced tax rates and aggressive tax avoidance. Indeed, corporate profits are the other area that has improved greatly in the past couple of decades, partly benefiting by offshoring jobs. The effective corporate tax rate could be raised back to 1 percent of GDP, adding another $140 billion to the coffers.[16]

Capital gains taxes, now set at a rate of 15 percent, could readily be raised to 28 percent on moderate to high-income individuals. This could raise $25 to $50 billion within a few years.[17]

There are other alternatives as well. A fifty cent tax on gasoline could raise $50 billion a year, for example.[18] Taxes on cigarettes or carbon emissions can also raise substantial money. A carbon tax could raise significant revenues and also reduce the use of electricity and other sources of carbon emissions. By one estimate, a tax that resulted in a 10 percent increase in the price of electricity would generate $40 billion in tax revenue a year.[19]

Such a combination of tax increases comes to $400 to $500 billion or so. Needless to say, not all should be advocated. Some of course overlap. One tax that many economists of varying political allegiances propose is a national sales tax or value-added tax. The advantage of such a tax is to reduce consumption by imposing taxes on purchases. Some advocate reducing income tax rates commensurately, thus raising incentives to work and invest. But such taxes are also regressive, taking more of the earnings of low-income than high-income workers. A system can be devised to provide credits to lower-income workers, however, though many believe it is inefficient. Proponents of the plan typically claim it is more favorable to rapid growth and investment than overall tax schemes that rely on incomes taxes, a controversial point we will not explore in this book. Nevertheless, such a tax has high revenue raising potential.[20] As Lindert has pointed out, most European nations depend more on such taxes than on income taxes.

■ ■ ■ ■ ■

As stated, the purpose of this book is not to propose a concrete detailed plan to raise revenue but to demonstrate the potential to raise moneys for government programs, and to loosen the nation from the artificial and binding belief that such taxing capacity is limited.[21]

But there is also room to spend money without using financing to support it. Budget deficits can be tolerated if the spending is directed to needed public investment. Such public investment has been so badly neglected that some, and possibly even much, of the spending will produce sufficiently faster income growth in coming years to equal the initial outlays in higher taxes and saved welfare expenditures. A great deal of interesting work has been done in a variety of fields to substantiate these claims. Such analyses should be seen as approximate at best, but they are telling.

In addition, the most productive way to address rising global competition is not trade restrictions per se but for the government to invest in the nation. Consumer spending leaks to foreign imports and business investment leaks across borders. But potential returns to the economy from spending on transportation projects are at this point significant, partly due to years of neglect, and the jobs created to implement them largely stay at home. The proportion of the federal budget spent on investment in the nation—including transportation, science, technology, and energy—are well down from the levels of the 1970s. Federal spending on education as a proportion of GDP fell under Clinton but was raised under his successor, George Bush, and it remains slightly higher as a proportion of GDP than it was in the 1970s. Overall, public investment equaled nearly 3 percent of GDP in the 1970s, which would come to more than $400 billion today. Under Clinton it fell to half of that proportion, and under Bush it rose but remains at less than 2 percent of GDP. Merely raising it to 1970s levels would produce $140 billion more a year to spend. To reemphasize, such spending usually creates domestic jobs and builds future productivity at the same time.

To take one estimate, a House Transportation Committee report cites a Federal Highway Administration model that claims that a $75 billion investment will create more than 3.5 million jobs and $464 billion in additional nationwide sales. Every $1 billion, in other words, yields 47,500 jobs and another $6 billion in sales.[22] Spending has been so inadequate that such estimates can be accepted confidently. The Society of Civil Engineers suggest that much of America's infrastructure should get a grade of D. While these studies are hardly definitive, they are suggestive of the possibilities.

The most exciting potential returns are for high-quality pre-K education. A wide range of studies has been undertaken on several high-quality programs that have long been underway in the United States. The benefits of such programs include not only improving the ability of children to learn, but also long-term reduction in crime rates, reduced need for special education and repeating grades, and lower welfare enrollment rates. A conventional conservative economist such as James Heckman, a Nobel laureate who opposes college subsidies, nevertheless favors significant funding of preschool programs.[23] Some estimate these programs create benefits that exceed costs by five to ten times.[24] A highly sophisticated recent analysis by two economists estimates that if a high-quality program was instituted nationwide, the federal moneys spent would be fully paid for in increased tax revenues due to improved incomes and would reduce welfare, crime, and special education expenses. In other words, it would pay for itself.[25]

In areas of energy investment, some analysts make similar claims. The Apollo Alliance—a consortium of business, environmentalists, and unions—argues that a program they have devised, costing $30 billion a year, would generate enough jobs and income to produce tax revenues that would fully reimburse the costs.

Such analyses are, like studies of how higher taxes limit growth, necessarily over-simplified. The causes of growth are complex and difficult to isolate, and they change under different economic and historical circumstances. Thus, all such studies are subject to fallacies of composition: it is hard to isolate single causes of growth. But so high are the suggested returns that they overwhelm the inherent weaknesses of such projections. Moreover, after so many years of neglect, these rates of return will be unusually high. History also strongly suggests that such spending will have a highly positive rate of return, or economic growth in America would not have been as rapid to begin with.

How can we think about such spending? I heard one well-known public economist proclaim at a closed session with House Democrats that we should remember that infrastructure spending is still spending. But it is not true. It is not throwing money away if it produces a rapid increase in GDP that otherwise would have been foregone. One simple way of thinking about public investment is to consider that every two dollars spent is adding over time one dollar in future tax revenues. This would be a conservative estimate given some analyses, which suggest a dollar of investment produces three or four dollars of future tax revenue over time. At the least, many of these programs will probably pay for themselves through additional tax revenues. For every $100 billion of public investment, then, we can think that only $50 billion will be added to a federal deficit. If we choose to be revenue neutral, we can think of its requiring only an additional $50 billion in tax revenues.

There are of course other ways to think of such investment. America can adopt a capital investment budget and separate it from its operating deficits. Some policymakers suggest an infrastructure bank to finance new projects. All of these and more should be on the table.

Finally, better regulation will have a cost. Even the most efficient of such regulations requires paperwork, corporate bureaucracy, and can slow competitive reaction or the introduction of new products. But analyses of the costs of such regulations, which were especially common in the 1980s when Reagan was president, have been remarkably one-sided. (Studies of environmental regulations are an exception, where benefits were weighed against costs, but these are highly controversial nevertheless.[26]) They almost always neglect or understate the benefits of regulation, which can be large. Had better regulation been in place that provided protection against the Enron scandals or the sub-prime credit crisis of 2007 and 2008, how much would the economy have benefited? The failure to understand fully the true role of regulation, especially in financial markets, is one of the key failures of this generation of public leadership. A reasonable analysis, however, must recognize that there are costs to regulation as well as benefits. Some regulation has been debilitating, but on balance it has been critical to the maintenance of prosperity.

America Has the Money

Not all problems or solutions are a function of money. If I neglect to discuss ways to improve government, streamline it, create incentives for efficiencies and performance, develop means of closing agencies and departments when they are no longer needed and reducing corruptions, it is not out of lack of concern. There is a tendency for government, like business monopoly or business lobbying power, to entrench itself and create inefficiencies and breed corruption. I also believe that flexible labor markets—flexible business in general—is imperative for growth and entrepreneurial vigor. This is an important reason why obligations such as health care and pensions, which impose a high cost per employee, are better managed by government—such a social structure will free business. The public discourse is so unbalanced against government, however, that my emphasis is necessarily on improvements to government.

As a consequence of neglect and change, an adequate agenda for America is a lengthy one, but it is not an antigrowth agenda. It favors growth. Growing personal income is more necessary to a full life than is recognized, in part because the cost of some key needs rise very fast, in part because a wealthy society can finance innovation, and in part because a wealthy populace will find it easier and more congenial to pay for communal needs through taxes. But for too long, mainstream economists have accepted the notion that more savings and technology will alone lead to faster growth. The agenda for government is therefore inappropriately limited; government spending, for example, will allegedly erode savings. America has been able to test this economic philosophy for a full generation and it has failed. Years of below-par productivity growth, low and stagnating wages, inattention to basic needs, persistent poverty, and the undermining of assets necessary to future growth, including education, health care, energy alternatives, and transportation infrastructure are the consequences.[27]

The gap between a growing economy and falling wages is the major contemporary mystery. Global competition and offshoring may explain part of the gap, but the trend began decades ago. Research shows that a gap in worker compensation and productivity began to open up slowly in the late 1980s: typical workers got less than their historical share, while capital (profits) and high-income workers got more. This gap widened explosively in the 2000s.[28]

Furthermore, there was little explanation as to why male incomes in particular fared especially poorly over this long period we have described. A major reason is the withdrawal of government from its traditional purposes.[29]

An Agenda

Given that economic growth is a prerequisite, and that government activity is not automatically detrimental to growth and often an important stimulus, let's more objectively get on with an agenda that in principle can right the nation. Below is a summary:

- The failure of wages to rise, even with rising productivity, must be directly addressed and no longer relegated to a natural law of economics that cannot be disturbed. Productivity rose rapidly in the early 2000s but wages, contrary to the free-market promise, stagnated. A serious minimum wage should be adopted in the nation, along with wage insurance for those who lose jobs through no fault of their own. Further subsidies should be studied, and expansion of the earned income tax credit and current unemployment insurance programs should be undertaken. Wage insurance is a double-edged sword because it may promote low-wage jobs, but should be considered.

- Global competition is best addressed through raising wages at home and significant public investment in infrastructure, energy, and education, which creates both domestic competitiveness and domestic jobs.
- The financial community must be re-regulated in cooperation with international partners. The basic principle should follow what it was throughout U.S. history. In the past, banks were the principal source of loans and the conduit between savings and investment. Eventually, they were regulated due to frequent financial instability and resulting deep recessions. Now the financial community has developed ways to channel savings and lever it so that it circumvents banks and therefore regulation. These institutions must now be controlled as if they were banks, with capital requirements and public disclosure responsibilities.
- The two-worker family has become the national norm, but the growth in single-parent families is also striking. Policies to support the needs of the new American family structures are vital to the nation's future.
- Health care costs rise significantly faster each year than individual or family income, and America pays far more per person than any other rich nation without cover-

ing all its citizens or performing as well as other nations. No financial need in coming decades will be more pressing. Both private and public medical spending will rise to a very high proportion of GDP. A universal health care system, efficiently reformed, is necessary.

■ College is today a requirement for a decent standard of living, just as primary school was in the 1800s and high school in the first half of the 1900s. It is a new cost in the march to the middle class, and a central asset of the economy. But the nation subsidizes much less of college expenses than it once did of primary and secondary schools. The nation requires a more significant subsidy of college for all who qualify.

■ K–12 education is too unequal in America. Through federal subsidy, spending per pupil must be equalized throughout the nation.

■ Pre-K education is now as much a necessity for the individual child, the family, and society as is K–12, and it should be a universal.

■ Caregivers in America earn too little money. The higher education of teachers, nurses, elder-care workers, and pre-K specialists must be subsidized more than for other students. Serious consideration should be given to higher minimum wages for such workers.

■ Vigorous antidiscrimination implementation is now necessary in America. Gender and racial differences are too widespread to be tolerated any longer. Affirmative action is just, and equal pay for equal work must be seriously implemented. Government contracts for services should be utilized to demand diversity and integration.

■ Energy use and transportation programs must be integrated under a single federal department. The nation's energy, so much of it for car and truck transport, can be organized much more efficiently. The transportation and water infrastructure of the nation is also decayed badly. But new transportation systems of greater efficiency, and urban and suburban planning, must be integrated with new gasoline taxes and subsidies for alternative fuels.

- The majority of election costs should be publically funded. Democracy is being undermined by the empowerment of special interests.

- Efforts to encourage trading partners overseas to adopt fair wage and environmental policies are now a requirement. Higher labor costs abroad will reduce the American competitive disadvantage and improve developing nations' domestic markets, beneficial both to developing nations and to exporters from America.

- All of the above are part of a strategy of economic growth. But such policies should also include recognizing that higher wages, which in turn raise consumer spending power, are also a serious and vital source of economic growth by creating demand for goods and services.[30]

In breadth, such an agenda is as ambitious as the New Deal, and some call for another New Deal. But there is a danger here. Much has changed. The New Deal was concerned with providing jobs for Americans. Now we know that a single job is often not good enough. The New Deal did little for African Americans. We now expect a far broader application of American rights and opportunities. We have medical treatments that are enormously expensive, and that people can and do live much longer than in the first half of the twentieth century, making retirement costs greater. We now know that investing in human capital is vital, if ever more expensive. This was barely considered in the New Deal. We now know that the world may at last be pressing up against its availability of natural resources. The list of change is long. In such a world, isn't it possible that government should be an even larger part of the GDP? Why is the nation aghast at this possibility? At the very least it must be debated.

An Agenda for the Nation: Addressing Low Salaries and Wages

The stagnation of salaries and wages is the heart of the matter. The nation can no longer afford to think unimaginatively about the issue. The problems involve a wide spectrum of workers, from the poor through the working poor, middle-income workers, and full-fledged middle-class workers. Several assumptions have proved wrong in recent decades.

First, economic growth has not raised all boats in America. As discussed in the previous sections, the top 10 percent, and even more so, the top 1 percent, have enjoyed income increases that are simply staggering compared to the rest of the nation. Sometimes workers rise into the higher levels, of course, but evidence now strongly shows that such income mobility is not higher than it was in the 1950s and 1960s when compensation for all workers rose more equally, and it has likely fallen for over the last two decades.[31] Moreover, the pool of wages and salaries for most Americans has grown more slowly than it has on a consistent basis since before the Civil War, due to long periods of slow productivity growth, higher levels of worker participation, and rising inequality.

Second, also as discussed earlier at greater length, getting a decent education is both harder to accomplish than once realized and does not necessarily solve the problem. It has become a necessary but not sufficient condition for advance to the middle class.

It is time to consider the following market interventions:

Progressive Income Taxes

Increasingly intense competition from low-wage manufacturers, especially in China and other parts of Asia, as well as India, are costing Americans jobs. Some consideration can be given to reduced taxes on lower-income Americans and the expansion of poverty programs. The costs are marginal. Under Bill Clinton, spending on poverty programs fell significantly as a proportion of GDP. Under Bush, ironically, they were raised slightly. Raising taxes on better-off Americans to finance programs for the poor are in a global world well justified.

Minimum Wage

Direct action is required. The minimum wage is more than 25 percent lower, adjusted for inflation, than it was in 1967. It has fallen to about 32 percent of the average wage compared to 45 percent of the average wage in the early 1970s. Women are affected most by a low minimum wage, and many workers are subject to it. In addition, minimum-wage workers contribute nearly 60 percent to their family incomes. Raising the minimum wage in steps by $2 to more than $7 per hour in 2009, as Congress legislated in the spring of 2007, is critical and will affect, according to some economists, up to 11 percent of the work force, mostly women, who are relegated in large numbers to low-pay work.[32]

The Living Wage

More than one hundred communities in America have now instituted a living wage. A movement that was odds-against has become a serious success. Largely, a living wage has been adopted by municipalities, who pay their workers such a minimum, and in some cases demand that their suppliers pay workers a minimum as well. An acceptable living wage can easily be double the minimum wage, according to its advocates. Sometimes it is even higher. Economist Robert Pollin has been a leader in this area, helping the city of Santa Monica pass a living hourly wage of $10.50 in 2002. The humanist proposal appears radical to a nation disposed against such interventions, but its purpose is to provide a family with a minimum by which to meet basic needs. Such budgets include medical care, decent housing rentals, and commuting expenses, but, for example, make no provision for vacations or dining out. The minimum wage of no more than $5 or even $6 or $7 in some states, does not nearly meet such basic needs.[33]

What is fascinating is that economic studies cited show the higher wages have not cost any appreciable number of jobs, as had been feared. If jobs have been lost, they have been modest. And even the increase in costs to municipalities due to higher pay has been modest at worst. Such studies do not adequately take into account the increase in buying power that may result from higher wages in the community, and that in turn stimulates economic growth in classical Keynesian ways. The federal government should take the lead in imposing high living wage demands for its own contracts.

Labor Organizing

Falling levels of unionization have significantly affected the wages of workers with only high school educations, particularly men. In the late 1980s, nearly 30 percent of workers were covered by union contracts compared to less than 14 percent today. For high school graduates, union representation fell from nearly 40 percent of such workers in 1978 to less than 20 percent today.[34] Union wages have always been significantly higher than nonunion wages, even in the same industries. Health care and pension benefits have been especially more generous for union than nonunion workers. Moreover, there is substantial evidence that higher wages and better benefits for union worker spill over to nonunion workers.

Declining unionization, however, is partly the result of the erosion of the industries in which unions were once strongest— typically industrial oligopolies. Deindustrialization has undermined big steel, big auto, and others in the rust belt. As profits declined in these industries, union contracts were increasingly difficult to afford and employment levels were difficult to maintain.

Deunionization is also, however, the result of direct political efforts. The National Labor Relations Act (NLRA) of 1935 was passed to enable workers to organize without undue threats from employers. But especially in the past three decades, studies show convincingly that employers have violated provisions of the Act time and again without adequate enforcement by the federal government. One such instructive study found that in 2002 in Chicago, one-third of companies surveyed fired workers when they tried to organize unions and two out of five threatened to close their operation or move if a union was formed. The acquiescence of the federal government has been the key factor in allowing business to wage its struggle against unions successfully. Many organizations have proposed reforms of the NLRA that are worth considering. At the very least, the law should be enforced and severe penalties imposed on violating companies. A reinvigoration of labor laws is necessary, not so much to strengthen the old unions, but to enable unions to grow in newer industries in which employees deserve more power. Retailing and health care are obvious examples. These services are in many respects the new giant industries in which market power accrues to employers. Unionization of such industries would significantly help raise wages without undue inefficiencies, but success in organizing new unions has been sporadic.[35]

By the same token, unions should not be relieved of serious responsibilities to be more inclusive of women and workers of color as well, as to understand the more tenuous nature of modern economic conditions. Enlightened unions in Europe have helped produce more prosperous economies by their willingness to share risks and burdens with the management of business. Unions bear no small responsibility for their increasing irrelevance in the nation.

Racial, Gender, and Sexual Discrimination

Racial and gender discrimination is by no means dead in America, and it contributes considerably to the slow growth of wages. In the case of racial bias, reality and perception are far apart. In a survey done several years ago, half of whites responded that they believed the nation had achieved racial equality but only one in five African Americans believed this was the case.[36] The evidence of racial discrimination is undeniable. One especially illustrative study was done by researchers at MIT and the University of Chicago in which they mailed job applications with identical resumes to companies, but half had characteristically African America names. Those with African America names attracted far fewer positive responses than the others.[37]

Moreover, differences in wages have remained high. As a proportion of white wages, black wages are only slightly higher than they were a generation ago. Women have closed the gap to some degree, but family incomes remain far apart on average. As noted, women of all races have enjoyed more rapid increases in incomes than men for a generation, but this may be due partly to their exploitation, to the further detriment of men—hiring them to do the same job at the lower wage. The public attitude that markets will somehow relieve the nation of discrimination is irresponsible in light of the facts. Moreover, noninterventionist attitudes have influenced the nation, many generally believing there is nothing to be done. This is untrue. Racial discrimination extends to housing and education. Indeed, neighborhoods are highly segregated again, as desegregation orders were reversed in the 1980s. Affirmative action programs are being successfully challenged, yet, though all such programs require sacrifices and incur social and economic costs, educators William Bowen and Derek Bok make strong arguments about the net benefits of these programs.[38]

Racial and gender discrimination is not inevitable. Gaps in pay, housing, education, and also criminal treatment can be closed. But the nation has been in retreat on these fundamental rights, and this can be reversed. As the nation becomes more sophisticated about the rights of the gay community, these too should be incorporated into any concern about nationwide discrimination. The market alone does not and cannot do the job. Public programs to hire minorities to do government work should be reinvigorated and expanded. Affirmative action should be retained and strengthened. Education should be equalized across communities. Women require protection from discrimination at work. Those discriminated against must have the right to take their grievances to court. Gays in America should have the right to marry.

A New Policy for Wage Guidelines

The poor performance of wages in an economy for three decades, despite GDP growth, suggests a chronic failure of the labor market. In the 2000s, in particular, profits have been strong without improving the standard of living for most workers. Many of the policies recommended above, including broader educational benefits, higher minimum wages and the imposition of living wages, more active collective bargaining, and an aggressive battle against discrimination, should begin to reverse the process through market interventions.

But it is also time to consider broad guidelines for wage growth throughout the nation. Public discussions between business, government, labor, and communities should be aggressively encouraged, and even required by law. For now, guidelines should not be mandated. But open discussion about wages with the interested parties, including local communities, and a full-scale report on impacts of business decisions on communities, can provide the public airing that brings attention to abuses of power. I include communities along with the customary triad of government, business, and labor because they are now so deeply affected by the closing of business due to changing technologies, foreign competition, and offshoring. Such a program could well be the most fruitful innovation in activating government again in a true partnership with business. Lessons, both good and bad, can be learned from European examples, despite inherent problems there as well.[39]

Trade, Offshoring, and Jobs

The argument in favor of free trade for a rich nation is a compelling one. Should we adopt quotas or tariffs to protect American businesses and jobs? The freedom to buy imported goods and to sell our own is also a central one, both to our freedom of choice and to our prosperity. On the other hand, lost jobs due to trade can so severely undermine buying power in America that it will inhibit rates of growth.

Many of the policies described above will reduce the disadvantage of the American worker. But further efforts are needed to eliminate artificial advantages companies have in moving jobs and operations abroad. Some move such operations abroad, for example, to take advantages of tax breaks rather than inherent cost or technological advantages. These should be leveled. An open discussion with the community of why job offshoring is taking place will also help force companies to make fully logical decisions rather than merely follow the pack.[40]

But as noted earlier, trade negotiations should now include efforts to raise labor and environmental standards with our trading partners. America should not be party to exploitation of either foreign workers or the local environment. By demanding worker and environmental safeguards, America would not be asserting its power but rather improving local societies while making American business more competitive. Giving priority to such a strategy over conventional protectionism does not rule out the possibility of applying tariffs to certain industries, but these policies should be used sparingly.

AN AGENDA FOR THE NATION: NEW SOCIAL
PROGRAMS AND PUBLIC INVESTMENT

The Two-worker Family: Early Education,
Day Care, and Family Leave

Nearly half of all families have two workers today. Moreover, these are the families whose incomes have risen, if only moderately. Families with only one worker have suffered most in the economy. Two-thirds of women work compared to only one-third at the midpoint of the twentieth century. A nation with a new social structure must support its people's needs with new institutions, just as it did in the past with primary schools, kindergartens, high schools, post offices, public hospitals, subways, and so on. Nowhere is the Reagan pessimism more evident than in the nation's refusal to build the institu-

tions necessary to support two-worker and single-parent families. The two-worker family is the consequence of pressure on
incomes and the justifiable ambitions of women to work and
have careers. The addition of women to the labor force is a
source of growth and not, on balance, a cost. But women must
be supported in order to maximize their contribution to the
economy, maintain the health of the family, and nourish their
personal lives.

Government should fund a full-time universal pre-K program for three- and four-year-olds. Such a nationwide program
would serve as a high quality day care service, which would
help free the spouse to work with less cost for quality care. It
would also contribute importantly to the welfare of many children, especially among the poor. There is a wide range of studies to support such claims, based on existing early child care
programs. As we noted in the previous section, children in
these programs are left back less frequently, require fewer special education services, generally earn more as adults and
therefore pay more taxes and contribute more productively to
the economy, and are less frequently dependent on federal
welfare programs. In fact, such programs may, when administered well, likely to pay for themselves by raising future incomes and tax revenues and reducing social costs. A study of
the federal Head Start program concludes that the social benefits of the program offset 40 to 60 percent of its costs. Such
programs also enable women to pursue their careers; they
broaden personal choice, and in turn enable women to contribute productively to the economy.

Work-friendly programs for women may well be important
sources of economic growth. Peter Lindert believes that European programs that encourage women to work and assure that
they will not lose their job or indeed their place in the work
hierarchy because they have had a child, have stimulated eco-

nomic growth generally because women can then fulfill more of their potential.[41] Two researchers, Marcia Myers and Janet Gornick, wrote in 2004 that they believe an ambitious child-care program that provides full-time care for three-to-five-year olds, and a part-time program for younger children, would cost roughly $110 billion a year. They also estimate that a six-month family leave program at full pay would cost nearly $50 billion a year if subsidized by the government. Such programs can be tailored in other ways, but a rough cost of $150 billion is a reasonable benchmark.[42]

Health Care for All

The need for a universal health care system is compelling on several key fronts. More than forty-five million Americans have no health insurance. Over two-thirds of the uninsured come from low-income families and over one-half are minorities. Half of the uninsured work full time. There is ample evidence that those without health insurance get inferior care on average. Preventive care is rare for such patients, and they often do not receive rudimentary treatment. One-third of the uninsured do not receive treatment when sick, despite access to public hospitals. A well-known study in the *New England Journal of Medicine* reported some years ago that 270,000 children with asthma do not see a doctor. A 2004 report from the Institute of Medicine shows that there are about 18,000 deaths each year of people under the age of sixty-five, due to the lack of health insurance, making it a leading cause of death. By comparison, there were 17,000 deaths due to diabetes and 19,500 due to stroke. A Kaiser Institute study indicates that providing health coverage to the uninsured would reduce the mortality of this group by 10 to 15 percent: "A reduction of this magnitude is comparable to the reduction in overall mortality over the last 40 years."[43] The resulting burden on public hospitals, partly due to lack of early attention, is enormous. And there are also convincing studies about how much poor health care costs the economy in terms of reduced worker productivity.

A second compelling reason for a single payer national health care system is the inefficiency of the American system, as measured by what Americans get from their health care services compared to the cost. America pays 15 percent of its GDP on health care compared to 9 percent in both Canada and France. In fact, America spends far more than any other nation in the world as a proportion of its incomes. But there is no evidence its outcomes are superior. According to the OECD, life expectancy in the United States is 77.2 years (2002–2003), lower than the OECD average of 78 years. Infant mortality has fallen but is still 7 deaths per 1,000 births, higher than the OECD average of 6.1 deaths per 1,000 births. The United States has the highest rate of obesity in the OECD at 30.6 percent of adults. On the other hand, we should not leap to the simplistic conclusion that American health care is by any means all poor. In terms of diagnosis and treatment, it does well in some areas, but not in others. Given the high level of resources devoted to it, the health care system should be incontestably superior to those abroad.[44]

A third reason for broad-scale reform is that health care coverage in America is largely dependent on one's job. A free nation can no longer assign responsibility for the health of the nation to employers, especially as international competition and new technologies threaten older industries. Even now, only two-thirds of companies with two hundred employees or more offer health insurance benefits; less than half with employees of twenty or fewer do so. Large companies are also under rising pressure. General Motors famously pays roughly $1,500 in health care benefits for every car it sells. The major

companies restrain wages to afford their health care obligations. And in general health care coverage is declining, and will
inexorably continue to do so.

The rapid rise in the cost of health services is the last and
most compelling reason for profound change in the health care
system. An estimate made by the Center for Medicare and
Medicaid Services is that the nation will spend 20 percent of
GDP on health care in ten years compared to approximately 15
percent today. Medicare and Medicaid costs will rise dramatically—much faster in fact than Social Security. Americans will
thus have to give up a lot to meet their medical bills, or they
will have to make an active choice for less health care—a
choice that would result in cruel triage, reducing or eliminating health care benefits for many. Again, a class divide in terms
of health, which already exists, will inevitably widen.

Some studies, including one by the Institute of Medicine,
show that a government financed system of health care with
control over prices, and shared and universal technology and
information services, can save the nation billions of dollars a
year. First, high administrative expenses would be reduced.
Second, computerized sharing of records would improve treatments and reduce common errors in treatment. Third, stan-
dardized clinical methods can be maintained. Finally, a coun-
tervailing power would be created to balance the market
control of pharmaceutical companies and hospitals. Such a system can also more efficiently create incentives for preventive
care, which is the best and least costly way to improve people's
health. A government-financed system can negotiate and help
control soaring drug prices, as well as other medical costs.

A single-payer system is considered politically impractical
in America. Huge insurance companies would become obso-
lete and hundreds of thousands of employees would lose their
jobs, an issue often neglected in the public discourse. There

have been many hybrid proposals about how to reform health care. Most attractive, in my view, is the broadening of Medicare to cover all Americans from its current program now limited to the elderly, advocated by Senator Edward Kennedy, among others. It would be fully financed through federal tax revenues. Such a program covers roughly 80 percent of doctor and out-patient costs for the elderly today and a high percentage of hospital costs.[45] Private plans are widely available, and with suitable regulation, can insure for the gaps in coverage. Universal Medicare could maintain choice of providers, and generally work the way traditional insurance has worked. It would enable the federal government to maintain significant levels of control without actually employing care-givers or running hospitals. Such a program would almost surely cost less than what Americans currently pay for medical care due to the savings mentioned above.

Nothing so reflects how dysfunctional the American political system is now than the inability to come to terms with the required reforms. Proponents are looked upon as naïve; given political realities, perhaps they are. But the nation's hand is increasingly being forced. Of all ironies in modern U.S. society, the greatest is that improving health care in America will probably cost Americans less—not more—than they now spend. Without broad reform, the nation faces much more serious triage in the distribution of adequate health services in coming decades.

K–College

The view that the American people should only support public education from kindergarten through high school is a costly anachronism. College today is not a guarantee but it is a necessary condition for a full life in America. Subsidizing college alone will not solve this problem. K–12 education must also be improved. This basic refusal of the nation to invest fully in its education is the classic example—the poster child—of a nation refusing to deal with change constructively.

Why? Because Americans believe they cannot afford it. In terms of college, reform has largely taken the form of making college loans available. Thus, critics of further subsidy fondly note that the true price of college is less than the sticker price. In fact, that true cost has been rising rapidly as well, and the results are record levels of debt for students when they graduate. Going on for an advanced degree adds more debt still. Rising costs of college, and the imperative for college, have divided America further along income lines. Qualified students from low-incomes families are far less likely to enroll in college than their higher-income counterparts.[46]

Social conditions are also critical as well, which makes universal pre-K all the more important. But full-fledged education programs that begin with early education seem an inescapable necessity for the new century. At least half of college tuition should be paid by the federal government for qualified students who are accepted by an accredited public institution—and an equivalent absolute amount for attendance at a private institution. Based on various estimates, this will cost on the order of $30 to $35 billion a year.[47] The federal government should devote another $25 billion toward equalizing educational opportunities by subsidizing K–12 teacher salaries in poorer regions of the nation. The correct approach toward improving K–12 requires not merely demanding higher standards through trial and error, but it also requires spending money.

Finally, the nation should in general subsidize the salaries of American caregivers by fully funding undergraduate and graduate programs for those who want to teach, go into nursing, or those who become day care or elder-care workers in accredited institutions. This can be funded generously at $25 billion a year.

Transportation

The nation's infrastructure has degenerated so badly that estimates of the costs for its renewal are simply overwhelming. When the American Society of Civil Engineers gives American infrastructure—including highways, airports, and water facilities—an average grade of D, it is simply difficult to respond.[48] Heating and cooling of buildings can also be far more efficient. A case can be made for spending even $200 billion a year more on infrastructure in America. If we keep in mind the likely returns on this investment, however, such spending is by no means unfathomable. As important, such spending creates domestic jobs.

The case I'd like to emphasize, however, is that Americans cannot treat transportation infrastructure in an isolated way any longer. Above all, infrastructure investment should be organized around energy and social needs. Cheap gas, low electricity costs, and unexploited land near big cities made an interstate highway system economically ideal by supporting the massive development of the suburbs. It probably accounted for more of American prosperity in those years than economists can capture with their statistical techniques. Today, we have expensive energy and electricity, high levels of pollution, and much longer commutes to the exurbs to find affordable housing. Energy and transportation policy can thus no longer be separated in America. It is a classic case for centralized and regionalized coordination, one of the key public goods historically provided by competent government. Separating such policymaking is a further example of outdated American practice—a failure to recognize change.

Currently, the United States, which represents only 5 percent of the world's population, accounts for 25 percent of the global demand for oil. In 2001 the United States consumed three times as much energy as China. Until the 1950s, the United States could supply its own energy needs. But by the end of that decade, we became net importers of energy. Some 55 percent of America oil is imported today and it is anticipated that 65 percent will be imported by 2020. Even when including coal and natural gas, 29 percent of energy usage in 2004 was from imports.[49]

America's use of oil has been largely driven by cars and trucks. People use their cars 88 percent of the time, while airline travel only accounts for 8 percent of personal travel. Between 1990 and 2003, vehicle travel on U.S. highways increased by 35 percent while the population only grew 17 percent. Over the longer period between 1970 and 2003, highway travel increased by 161 percent and the population grew 43 percent.[50]

Commodities are transported using a variety of methods, including air carriers, barges, and freight trains. But trucks carry by far the largest proportion of goods, nine or ten times more in value than that transported by air, rail, and ship combined. Congestion, which has increased significantly, is costly to the nation, creates more demand for gasoline, and exacerbates pollution.

Individual Americans spend $54 billion a year in car repairs and operating costs due to damage caused by poor road conditions. Furthermore, congestion has increased over the past decade, increasing the average 25.8 minute trip (in traffic in 1987) to 30 minutes in 2000. It is estimated that increased traffic costs Americans $63.1 billion in wasted time and fuel costs. Poor road conditions may also account for 30 percent of traffic fatalities, or close to 13,000 deaths in 2004.

Public transport and rail are vital in reducing congestion, pollution, and commuting times in urban areas—and they typically use far less energy per mile. Such transport is essential for many poor and middle-income families to commute to work and school. Some 90 percent of public assistance recipients do not own cars. However, transit railways have decreased in average speed and now experience more delays as well, largely reflecting the increased demand for commuter trains and rail travel.[51]

If the demands are high, it is also clear that such investment has substantial economic pay-offs. The academic literature strongly supports the conclusions that there is a significant economic return to such investment.[52] The issue is choosing appropriate projects. The level of optimal spending is probably high, much higher than current spending. It seems fair to ask motorists to support such changes through higher gasoline or carbon taxes, though such a tax falls unevenly on industries and regions that use more energy, and adjustments are required.

Ideally, energy policy, transportation policy, and urban development should be merged in a single federal cabinet agency. At the least, energy and transportation should be merged. Energy efficiency requires rail transportation, more enlightened urban and suburban planning, and subsidies for efficient residential and commercial instruction.

The Apollo Alliance has attracted considerable attention in Washington for policy proposals along these lines, and their work provides a useful model. The Apollo Alliance project focuses its efforts largely on investment in alternative fuels, hybrid cars, fuel-efficient buildings, and fuel-efficient transportation. The group proposes that $30 billion a year should be spent on these projects over ten years. From this investment, based on a complex econometric model, they calculate that over ten years, 3.3 million jobs will be created and $1.4 trillion in new GDP will be generated. They estimate that by 2015, 38 percent of cars driven in America can be hybrid or hydrogen cars and 15 percent of the country's electrical needs can be met by renewable energy sources. Additionally, their plan will reduce energy consumption by 16 percent overall through greater efficiencies. Apollo figures that their programs can reduce Persian Gulf oil imports by at least half and potentially entirely.

On balance, Apollo argues that such a program will reduce costs and generate production and jobs sufficient to pay for itself over time. They believe that investing in technologies such as wind power, solar power, hydrogen fuel cells, and efficient automobiles will generate new industries—much like government investment in NASA, highways, and railroads historically helped to generate new industries in high technology and transportation. Subsidies for building green buildings or retrofitting existing buildings can generate new construction jobs. Improving electricity transmission can create more maintenance and operations jobs. Subsidizing hybrid car manufacturing can help ailing carmakers hire more workers instead of laying off existing workers. Apollo also finds that energy efficiency is typically labor intensive. For every $1 million of investment, they estimate that 21.5 jobs are created—$1 billion would create 21,500 jobs. For every $1 million invested in natural gas generation, by comparison, only 11.5 jobs are created. Investing in renewables, Apollo calculates, creates 40 percent more jobs than investing the same amount in coal.[53]

Overall, Apollo makes a cogent argument that the $300 billion investment over ten years will generate $307 billion in federal tax revenues, and they also anticipate an increase in personal income of $953 billion. Apollo can serve as a model for government investment. America is the world's major oil consumer, but growing demand from newly developing nations, as widely reported, such as China, will put added pressure both on fossil fuels and on the environment. Energy, transportation, and urban policies should be integrally linked with environmental policies and international issues.

I present this only as a guideline. Senators Chris Dodd and Charles Hagel introduced sensible legislation in 2007 to establish a federal bank to guarantee bonds in support of specific infrastructure projects. Thus, budget outlays are minimized. Given the likely high returns from such projects, such a proposal makes good sense. But funded at $60 billion initially, it seems too little. The nation may well need to make another $50 billion a year in such investments. For our purposes, we should delegate $50 billion in total per year for infrastructure and energy projects, with the expectation that much more spending can be supported through an infrastructure bank. Serious coordination is urgent, as is the development of infrastructure priorities. As I write this, the infrastructure discourse is fragmented and overgeneralized.

An Expanded Safety Net for the Times

Social Security

The reader may wonder why I have not treated Social Security at length. But a nation willing to make appropriate investments in its future will have less difficulty than is realized in raising taxes sufficiently to make Social Security whole. In fact, the risks to Social Security have been dramatically exaggerated. An aging society will have consequences, as there are fewer people of working age to support both the retired and children. But long-term estimates of the gap between Social Security taxes and future outlays are based on fairly cautious assumptions. Even then, the gap comes to no more than 1 percent of GDP a year over time. In 2007, this would have amounted to about $120 billion.

The problem is that the shortfall may have to be faced sooner than is expected. Social Security could well begin to be a drag on federal spending in ten or twelve years. Even then, it will not require large levels of additional finance. A nation with a $14 trillion GDP and more than $40 trillion in personal assets after liabilities can readily afford it.

But Social Security is no longer enough at a time when American corporations have shifted boldly and recklessly from guaranteeing pension benefits to a system in which the worker is largely responsible for saving for his or her own retirement, with employer contributions as a supplement. The adequacy of retirement in the future, dominated by discussions about the solvency of Social Security, has missed the forest for the trees. First, reforms to Social Security that already exist, including a higher retirement age, will reduce the future payout of benefits as a proportion of preretirement income. Second, the aggressive movement from defined benefits to defined contribution plans such as 401(k)s will almost surely leave many of the elderly more vulnerable. This is a source of controversy today, but the evidence is growing clear. Future retirees will save too little and manage their moneys poorly, even with the tax deferments available on contributions. Third, and most important, half of American workers have no private pension program; they are largely dependent on Social Security benefits for their retirement.

Some economists, like Alicia Munnell of Boston College, argue that we must impose higher retirement ages on the elderly. This can dramatically reduce retirement needs by increasing savings and also reducing the years of retirement. Others, like Teresa Ghilarducci and Robin Blackburn, believe such an increase would be cruel and impractical. Ghilarducci proposes that higher levels of savings be mandated by the federal government. To help poorer workers, she proposes paying them subsidies by eliminating the tax preferences for future contributions to plans like 401(k)s. These more radical proposals will attract political opposition, but we should understand that retirement security of the elderly now involves more than making Social Security solvent.

One counterintuitive but appealing possibility over time may be to expand Social Security significantly by raising payroll taxes on individuals and business progressively, and thereby providing benefits much more progressively as well. Lower-income workers could be paid a much higher proportion of the pre-retirement incomes, for example, and not have to meet current obligations for longevity on the job.[54]

Unemployment Insurance

Unemployment insurance, which was created in 1935, is a central component of the government's safety net. In the 1960s, Ronald Reagan famously called unemployment insurance a pre-paid vacation for freeloaders. During his presidency, he successfully narrowed its coverage, reducing both the proportion of workers covered and the amount paid on average. Given the tumultuous nature of the economy over this period, such callousness was remarkably insensitive in retrospect.

The unemployment insurance system, largely managed by the states, provides a remarkable and underutilized framework for expanding the nation's safety net efficiently. But today in many states only one in three jobless Americans qualify for unemployment insurance. The structure of the workforce has changed dramatically, as we have discussed at length. Women in particular are at a disadvantage in a system based on the male as the breadwinner, as they often take part-time work to make ends meet. The system must expand with the times to cover more temporary and part-time workers, more low-wage workers, and benefits for family hardships. Similarly, workers remain unemployed for longer periods of times these days and coverage should be extended from the existing thirteen weeks. Such an expansion is in fact not very costly and could be accomplished for less than additional $25 billion a year.[55]

Trade Adjustment Assistance Programs

In 1974, America passed a program to help those who lose jobs due to international competition. The program has been expanded since and provides weekly unemployment compensation and serious funding for job training.[56] But it requires reform. For one thing, the program is not well-known to those who may qualify for assistance. Its benefits should also be expanded. Most important, the number of industries in which jobs are lost due to trade must be expanded realistically. Effective expansion of this program would require spending another

TABLE 9

Spending on Labor Market
Adjustment Programs

	As a Percentage of GDP
Canada	0.41
France	1.32
Germany	1.21
Japan	0.28
United Kingdom	0.37
United States	0.15

Source: OECD, Employment Outlook 2003, Table 4.2, Indicators for Spending on Active Labour Market Programs, p. 139.

$10 billion a year, according to the Institute for International Economics. The proposal to expand existing unemployment insurance mentioned above totals less than $15 billion a year. Extending unemployment insurance another thirteen weeks would cost roughly $7 billion. Today, America spends significantly less as a proportion of GDP on these two functions than do other rich nations, as can be seen in the table.

Doubling America's commitment to 0.30 percent of GDP would provide significantly improved benefits in a time of serious job dislocation and uncertainty. The nation could easily consider more generous options.

AN AGENDA FOR THE NATION: NEW REGULATIONS

The Re-regulation of Finance

The modern age of financial regulation began with the New Deal. The excesses and corruption of the 1920s stunned the nation. The failure of thousands of banks caused untold Americans to lose their savings. Regulations were established to raise the transparency of these markets, to reduce conflicts of interest, and to limit the extension of credit. Beginning in the 1960s, these began to be reversed, sometimes correctly but often aggressively and with little thought to the inherent problems of deregulated finance.

Eventually, without regulation or oversight, history tells us that financial markets lead to excess, manipulation, and corruption. Overvalued stocks, housing, and other assets result in the inefficient allocation of capital and unwarranted rewarding of perverse economic behavior.

In today's markets, there are countless new investment and hedging vehicles and strategies. Financial markets are also completely international today. Re-regulating markets is thus a major undertaking, which will require more intense international cooperation that ever before.

Will there be a cost? Yes, in red tape and bureaucratic sluggishness, but there will also be enormous benefits in openness, freer competition, and fair practices. This book is not the place to propose a global financial blueprint. But one principle is clear. Commercial banks, which were regulated largely under the auspices of the Federal Reserve and the Comptroller of the Currency, are no longer the sole creators of credit. Other institutions, notably investment banks, should also be brought under similar regulation with minimum standards for capital, practice, and public disclosure.

The Public Financing of Elections

I could not have imagined as a young man in America in the 1970s that I would be concerned about the vitality of America's democracy. Certainly not about voting rights. So much progress had been made in the 1960s to guarantee suffrage to African Americans, after a couple of centuries of abuse. Similarly, affirmative action and other new programs were being implemented, even if the Equal Rights Amendment to the Constitution hadn't been passed.

But America backtracked unpredictably. The 2006 elections were fraught with accusations about fraudulent voting machines. During the Bush Administration, aggressive stands were taken to narrow the voting rights of African Americans to vote, including attempts to require driver's licenses to vote. The rising influence of moneyed vested interests over lawmakers represents the greatest threat—of an ideological faith in the free market—in protecting freedom in America. The purpose of government is too easily undermined. The *Washington Post* reported in 2005 that the number of federal lobbyists had risen from more than 16,000 to more than 34,000 just since 2000, and the money spent on lobbying exceeded $2 billion.[57]

■ ■ ■ ■ ■

In the closing pages of this book, it's worth summarizing several of the key contributions to prosperity, and the furtherance of personal freedom and equality that democracy facilitated. Economists like Peter Lindert think of democracy as giving people "voice," and he argues it was the moving force behind the free primary education system. The rise of democracy during the Jackson period protected and furthered the ownership of land and competition through the distribution of corporate charters. A rising democracy resulted in worker protection laws, a progressive income tax, and undergirded the New Deal. I would argue that the democratic spirit led to the proliferation of newspapers, relatively free speech, and broad access to information in America. Some will argue that democracy also led to overspending by government and inflationary policies. These latter problems in America's history, and that of all rich nations, have been the lesser of the evils. Democracy's economic benefits outweigh its disadvantages. All rich nations of the West and most in the East are democracies. Some are challenging that proposition today, including China and Russia, finding that central direction is the quicker path to benefits. This is one of the experiments of the age, but restricted information alone, so common to these authoritarian nations, will impede growth. Friedman in *Capitalism and Freedom* almost never mentions democracy and certainly does not propose that it was a guarantor of the personal freedom he cherished, an odd issue to overlook. At the point of his writing, his greater fear was the will of a "temporary majority." But economic necessity itself may further democracy in many nations.

The theme requires a book-length treatment in itself, but we have discussed clear examples of how critical democracy has been to prosperity and the distribution of property and income in America.

Ideally, national campaigns in America should be financed publicly. In 2006, one estimate by the *Wall Street Journal* was that roughly $2.5 billion would be spent on campaigning for national office. In an age of advertising overkill, and even at this level, the nation could readily set aside even such sums to free qualified candidates from loyalty to rich vested interests. Many organizations have dedicated resources to studying and proposing plans to implement public financing of elections, to which I can add little. But it is the first important step in preserving a democracy that represents the people.

A National Agenda: Growth

No major nation in history has depended on economic growth as much as the United States has to solve its social problems. This is different from depending on free markets. Economic growth, as defined earlier, is the constant expansion of GDP— the amount of goods and services the nation produces each year. Such production, in turn, produces the income of its people and businesses—their wages and salaries, profits, interest, and rental income. As the economy grows, so incomes grow. Is this income distributed reasonably? That is another matter. But due to a partnership of free markets and government efforts, regulation and investment, with democracy and open access to information as a foundation, the American standard of living grew remarkably rapidly even in the 1800s and still faster in the 1900s. There were many hardships and deep recessions, but time and again the economy burst forth from recession to produce higher wages, salaries, and profits. So broad was the dispensation of this bounty that a true class consciousness was never formed, even if in reality there were forms of class division and conflict. Rapid economic growth allowed America to solve its problems, not without government, but with less government than in other comparably rich nations. Rising income from rapid growth served as the foremost of the nation's social policies. As Alan Brinkley has shown, the New Deal spirit was abandoned early in favor of an emphasis on rapid growth of the economy after World War II. But in my view, this could occur only because the benefits of rapid growth over the next several decades were shared widely.[58]

Rapid economic growth remains among the nation's most potent weapons for spreading of opportunity, freedom, and democracy. Almost all the programs cited above will, if implemented wisely and to a reasonable extent, expand prosperity, not detract from it. Education, urban planning, and efficient energy use, health care for all—these are the foundations of a new and inclusive prosperity. Fiscal and monetary policies can support faster growth by becoming less fixated on inflation. A modest rise in the inflation target will generate significant prosperity.

But what of rising wages subsidized by government policies? They have been too readily treated as a cost of doing business rather than a source of growth through increases in buying power. Wages can become excessively high, but they are not nearly so in modern America.[59]

What are the costs of the programs above? Excluding reforms of health care, which will likely pay for themselves, they come to roughly an additional $400 billion a year.

This is 3 percent of GDP today, which as I argue, can be paid out of tax increases as necessary. I also argue that some of it can be borrowed, producing somewhat higher federal budget defi-

TABLE 10
A Budget for the Nation's Improvement

Pre-K	150
College subsidies	35
K-12	25
Caregiver support	25
Infrastructure/energy	50
Social Security solvency	120
Unemployment expansion/Trade Assistance program	25
Election financing	2.5
Total	$432.5 billion

cits. Many of these programs will generate substantial tax revenues in the future—some of them more than they cost. Thus the short-term bill is misleading. It is far less.

To implement health care reform may require an additional $100 billion in the short run than I quantify here, but much if not all of this will be saved as reforms are implemented and efficiencies improved. I do not include additional mandated savings or higher taxes for retirement. This is a subject the nation should consider carefully, but it could be financed by reducing tax advantages that are now provided for programs like 401(k)s that are largely enjoyed by better-off Americans.

We today believe such an investment in the nation is immoderate only because we have been told for too long that it is. Three percent of GDP reinvested in the nation can buy America a fair and prosperous society, a free and optimistic society, and give the country a renewed lease on one of the great social experiments in the history of mankind.

■ ■ ■ ■ ■

Growth itself, without serious all-encompassing response from government, will simply not guarantee a prosperous and free society. Government has not responded to changed conditions. Business, remarkable in many ways, has in significant measure become abusive of workers again. Meanwhile, social and public goods are neglected to the point of tragedy. But a fearful nation reads its history poorly—looks backward to minimal government rather than forward to pragmatic change, and thinks itself in financial straits rather than rich and privileged. The unfolding of American history will not automatically follow its best earlier examples. Writers alarm the public merely by telling it how large government is. A complex economy requires such a government to function. Modest policy change will not be adequate. As I've said, it reflects a willful misreading of history. It is not the political center that has been vital in America but those quite remarkable political thrusts into unproven, risky, and even occasionally radical social territory. The pendulum does not inevitably swing back far enough or fast enough.

NOTES

··············

PART I

GOVERNMENT AND CHANGE IN AMERICA

1. Fred Thompson, "Closed Case: Tax Cuts Mean Economic Growth," *The Wall Street Journal,* April 4, 2007, p. A22.

2. Dick Armey, speech, Feb. 1, 2007, http://www.freedomworks.org/informed/issues_template.php?issue_id=2889.

3. Stephen Rose, "What's Not the Matter with the Middle Class," *The American Prospect,* Sept. 4, 2006, http://www.prospect.org/cs/articles?articleId=11943.

4. Milton Friedman, *Capitalism and Freedom* (Chicago: University of Chicago Press, 1962 2002), p. vi.

5. William Greider, *The Secrets of the Temple: How the Federal Reserve Runs the Country* (New York: Simon & Schuster, 1989), p. 218.

6. Friedman's central contention was that a growing money supply created inflation, but it was government spending that in these times usually caused excessive creation of money. It is now a highly contentious proposition. His direct case against government was more ideological than empirical, by and large arguing that any government interference was bound to make the market mechanism less efficient, even for social goods and services. Alan Blinder showed convincingly that the growth of the money supply in no way anticipated the rapid rise of inflation, however, undermining Friedman's claims. Alan S. Blinder, *Economic Policy and Great Stagflation* (New York: Elsevier Science & Technology Books, 1981).

7. Elizabeth Holmes and Amy Chozick, "Bruised in Iowa, Clinton, Romney Change Styles," *The Wall Street Journal,* January 7, 2008, p. A1.

8. Peter Lindert, *Growing Public: Social Spending and Economic Growth*

Since the 18th Century (NewYork: Cambridge University Press, 2004), p. 227.

9. Garry Wills, *A Necessary Evil: A History of American Distrust of Government* (NewYork: Simon & Schuster, 2002).

10. See in particular, Amartya Sen, *Development As Freedom* (New York: Knopf, 1999).

11. Incomes for women rose in this period, but at moderate rates, and the gap between male and female incomes narrowed but remained high. More female labor participation did not, therefore, result in substantially higher family incomes over time. See ibid.

12. On public discourse in democracies, see ibid.

13. Ibid., p. 30.

14. Ibid., p. 43.

15. Martin Feldstein, "American Economic Policy in the 1980s: A Personal View," in *American Economic Policy in the 1980s.*, ed. Martin Feldstein (Chicago: University of Chicago Press, 1994), p. 1.

16. Joel Slemrod and Jon Bakija, *Taxing Ourselves: A Citizen's Guide to the Great Debate OverTax Reform* (Boston: MIT Press, 2001), pp. 130–31.

17. Such analysis was made possible by new data sets only created starting in the late 1970s. Irving B. Kravis, AlanW. Heston, and Robert Summers (1978). "Real GDP Per Capita for MoreThan One Hundred Countries," *Economic Journal*, 88(350), pp. 215–42. *(Abstract from JSTOR.)*

18. Joel Slemrod, "What Do Cross-Country Studies Teach about Government Involvement, Prosperity, and Economic Growth," Brookings Papers on Economic Activity, 2:1995, pp. 373, 471.

19. Lindert, *Growing Public*, pp. 21, 30, 17.

20. Peter. H Lindert, "Welfare States, Markets and Efficiency: The Free Lunch Puzzle," working paper presented atVan Leer Jerusalem Institute, Dec. 2007, pp. 5–6.

21. Lindert, *Growing Public*, p. 233. See pp. 227–35 for a summary of the key literature.

22. Lindert, "Wefare States," p. 5.

23. Jonas Pontusson, "Whither Social Europe?," *Challenge Magazine*, November/December 2006.

24. Lawrence Mishel, Sylvia Allegretto, and Jared Bernstein (eds.), *The State of Working America, 2006/2007* (Ithaca, NY: Cornell University Press, 2006), Table 8.7, p. 334.

25. See Pontusson, "Whither Social Europe?" The Nordic model deliberately compresses wages, Pontusson notes, thus keeping up low-end wages in order to reduce the number of low-productivity jobs, and keeping down higher-end wages to raise the number of high-productivity jobs. The Nordic labor model is also more flexible than Europe's, reducing costs per worker—with the idea, not of making any job secure, but making the entire labor market secure.

26. Lindert, *Growing Public*, p. 282.

27. Mishel et al., *The State of Working America*, pp. 332–42.

28. Price V. Fishback and Robert Higgs (eds.), *Government and the American Economy: A New History* (Chicago: University of Chicago Press, 2007), p. 523.

29. The U.S. Bureau of the Census, *The Statistical Abstract of the United States, 2008*. Tables 460 and 461. Additional analysis, Larry Littlefield, http://www.r8ny.com/files/Federal%20Revenues%20and%20Expenditures%201979%20to%202006.xls.

30. Long-term historical data based on Angus Maddison, *Monitoring the World Economy, 1820–1992* (OECD, 1995).

31. The OECD Social Expenditures Database, 1980–1996, in Lindert, *Growing Public*, p. 13.

32. Armey, speech, Feb. 1, 2007.

33. Richard Brookhiser, *What Would the Founders Do? Our Questions, Their Answers* (New York: Basic Books, 2006).

34. Lewis K. Uhler, *Setting Limits: Constitutional Control of Government* (Washington, D.C.: Regnery Publishing, Inc., An Eagle Publishing Company, 1990).

35. Antonin Scalia, remarks at The Woodrow Wilson International Center for Scholars in Washington, D.C., March 14, 2005.

36. Stephen Breyer, the Supreme Court justice, has written a fine defense of an opposing point of view, arguing that court decisions must deal with a changing society, in *Active Liberty, Interpreting Our Democratic Constitution* (New York: Random House, 2005).

37. See in general, Isaiah Berlin, "Two Concepts of Liberty," in *Four Essays on Liberty*, ed. I. Berlin (New York: Oxford University Press, 1969).

38. Friedman, *Capitalism and Freedom*, p. 15.

39. Quoted in Eric Foner, *The Story of American Freedom*, (New York: Norton, 1999), p. 287.

40. Roosevelt's economic bill of rights. Samuel Rosenman, ed., *The Public Papers & Addresses of Franklin D. Roosevelt*, Vol XIII (New York: Harper, 1950), pp. 40–42

41. Foner, *The Story of American Freedom*.

42. Neil Gilbert, *The Transformation of the Welfare State: The Silent Surrender of Public Responsibility* (New York: Oxford University Press, 2002).

43. See Part II of Jacob S. Hacker's fine historical analysis, *The Divided Welfare State* (New York: Cambridge University Press, 2002), pp. 179–269.

44. See Gordon S. Wood, preface, in *Liberty, Property and the Foundation of the American Constitution*, eds. Ellen Frankel Paul and Howard Dickman (Albany: State University of New York Press, 1989), p. xii.

45. Quote and citation by William Letwin, "The Economic Policy of the Constitution," in ibid., p. 130.

46. Ibid., pp. 123–26.

47. Ibid., pp. 134–35.

48. Joyce Appleby, Arthur M. Schlesinger (eds.), *Thomas Jefferson* (The American President Series) (New York: Times Books, 2003), p. 97.

49. Quoted in Frank Bourgin, *The Great Challenge: The Myth of Laissez Faire in the Early Republic* (New York: Harper & Row, 1989), p. 132.

50. Ibid., p. 125.

51. Ibid., p. 116

52. Edward Chase Kirkland, *History of American Economic Life* (New York: Prentice Hall, 1969), pp. 83–85.

53. Allan Kulikoff, *The Agrarian Origins of American Capitalism* (Charlottesville: University Press of Virginia, 1992), p. 45.

54. For an excellent summary, see Price Fishback, et al., *Government and the American Economy* (Chicago: University of Chicago Press, 2007), pp. 94–115.

55. Quoted in Bourgin, *The Great Challenge*, p. 135.

56. Quoted in Appleby, *Thomas Jefferson*, p. 89

57. Bourgin, *The Great Challenge,* p. 135.

58. Wills, *A Necessary Evil*, p. 377.

59. Quoted by Drew R. McCoy, *The Elusive Republic: Political Economy in Jeffersonian America* (Chapel Hill: University of North Carolina Press, 1996), p. 110.

60. Bourgin, *The Great Challenge*, p. 169.

61. Charles Sellers, *The Market Revolution: Jacksonian America, 1815–1846* (New York: Oxford University Press, 1991), p. 39.

62. Sean Wilentz, *The Rise of American Democracy: Jefferson to Lincoln* (New York: Norton, 2006), p. 520.

63. Sellers, *The Market Revolution*, p. 40.

64. Ibid.

65. Ibid.

66. Gordon S. Wood, *The Radicalism of the American Revolution* (New York: Knopf, 1991), pp. 320–21.

67. For an updated view, see Robert P. Merges, "Who Owns the Charles River Bridge? Intellectual property and competition in the Software Industry," Boalt Working Papers in Public Law (paper 64, 1999), http://repositories.cdlib.org/cgi/viewcontent.cgi?article=1066&context=boaltwp (last visited Nov. 11, 2007).

68. Sellers, *The Market Revolution*, pp. 367–69.

69. Lindert, *Growing Public*, pp. 88–99.

70. Foner, *The Story of American Freedom*, p. 59. Foner cautions that wage labor was an ambiguous term, since full-fledged industrial armies of manufacturing workers hardly existed in Lincoln's time. It was the historically small business that still dominated in the new economy then.

71. Alfred Chandler, *Scale and Scope, the Dynamics of Industrial Capitalism* (Cambridge: Belknap Press, 1990).

72. Wilentz, *The Rise of American Democracy*.

73. Thomas Bender, *A Nation Among Nations: America's Place in World History* (New York: Hill & Wang, 2006), p. 139.

74. Ibid.

75. Garry Wills, *Lincoln at Gettysburg: The Words that Remade America*

(New York: Simon and Schuster,, 1992), in general and especially pp. 144–47.

76. Ibid., p. 158

77. Foner, *The Story of American Freedom*, p. 107.

78. *Plessy v. Ferguson*, 1896, ibid., p. 132.

79. Fishback, et al., *Government and the American Economy*, pp. 261–62.

80. Foner, *The Story of American Freedom*, p. 113.

81. Census Bureau, *Historical Statistics of the United States: Earliest Times to the Present*, (New York: Cambridge University Press, 2006), Table Bb9–56.

82. Environmental Protection Agency website (http://www.epa.gov/msw/timeline_alt.htm [last visited Oct. 21, 2007]).

83. Laurie Garrett, *Betrayal of Trust: The Collapse of Global Public Health* (New York: Hyperion, 2001).

84. Fishback, et al., *Government and the American Economy*, pp. 276–78.

85. U.S. Department of Treasury Fact Sheet, http://www.treas.gov/education/fact-sheets/taxes/ustax.shtml

86. Foner, *The Story of American Freedom*, Chapter 8, pp. 163–93.

87. Ibid., p. 184.

88. Ira Katz Nelson, *Liberalism's Crooked Circle* (Princeton, NJ: Princeton University Press, 1998).

89. David C. Mowery and Nathan Rosenberg, *Paths of Innovation: Technological Change in Twentieth Century America* (New York: Cambridge University Press, 1998), chapter 4 in general.

90. Foner, *The Story of American Freedom*, p. 192

91. Alicia Haydock Munnell and Steven A. Sass, *Social Security and the Stock Market: How the Pursuit of Market Magic Shapes the System* (Kalamazoo, MI: W.E. Upjohn Institute for Employment Research), pp. 24–27.

92. Jaocb Hacker, *The Divided Welfare State: The Battle over Public and Private Social Benefits in the United States* (New York: Cambridge University Press, 2002).

93. United States Department of Veteran Affairs, http://www.gibill.va.gov/GI_Bill_Info/history.htm (last visited Dec. 4, 2007).

94. Dwight D. Eisenhower Memorial Commission, http://www.eisenhowermemorial.org/social-security.htm, (last visited Dec. 5, 2007).

95. Fishback, et al., *Government and the American Economy*, p. 519.

96. Mowery and Rosenberg, *Technology and the Pursuit of Economic Growth*.

97. Friedman, *Capitalism and Freedom*, pp. 31–32.

98. There is a large literature, especially among Austrian economists, on principles of coordination through markets. Some of this argues that government is inefficient at coordination. I find it remarkably unconvincing. There is a counterliterature revolving around clusters and informal networks in business.

99. Jeff Madrick, "Breaking the Stranglehold on Growth," Agenda for Shared Prosperity, Economic Policy Institute, June 27, 2007 (EPI Briefing Paper #192).

100. Descendants of Friedman since renounced any capabilities of such policies to influence the business cycle. In turn, there has been a more recent reaction against them.

PART II
How Much We Have Changed

1. In general, growth models based on the work of Robert Solow, for which he won a Nobel Prize, emphasized at first technology and then other "supply-side" factors, such as education and research and development. It became clear that what was originally isolated as technological advance was a catch-all variable, which included many other factors, some of them admittedly unknown. Still, many economists argue that technological advance is a first among equals, which probably states the case at least in my view, much too strongly. Indeed, demand and the size of markets, in particular domestic markets, are critical to growth and have been badly neglected in recent research. In a classic work, Nathan Rosenberg summarized what I think is a reasonable position: "Rather than viewing either the existence of a market demand or the existence of technological opportunity as each representing a sufficient condition for innovation to occur, one should consider them each as necessary, but not sufficient, for innovation to result." *Inside the Black Box* (New York: Cambridge University Press, 1982),

pp. 231–32. As an example of the broadening of the conditions thought necessary for growth, see in particular the recent research on the importance of institutions such as law and finance for growth. In my view, this literature is again too narrow. But a good summary of the many factors can be found in William Easterly's book on development economics, *The Elusive Quest for Growth: Economists' Adventures and Misadventures in the Tropics* (Cambridge: MIT Press, 2001). An updated summary can be found in *The White Man's Burden: How the West's Efforts to Aid the Rest Have Done So Much Ill and So Little Good* (New York: Penguin, 2006). This is not to endorse Easterly's central conclusions, however, because they give too little credit to factors such as foreign aid, public investment, and large markets. For a counterview suggesting that aid, appropriately applied, can work, see Camelia Minoiu and Sanjay Reddy, "Aid Matters: Revisiting the Relationship between Aid and Growth," *Challenge Magazine*, March/April, 2007.

2. Murray Rothbard, *The Panic of 1819* (New York: Columbia University Press, 1962).

3. Charles P. Kindleberger, Robert Z. Aliber, and Robert Solow, *Manias, Panics, and Crashes: A History of Financial Crises* (Hoboken, NJ: Wiley, 2005).

4. There are many sources, including Alfred Chandler's remarkable economic histories, but one of the newer well-done works is Vaclav Smil, *Creating the Twentieth Century: Technical Innovations of 1867–1914 and Their Lasting Impact* (New York: Oxford University Press, 2005). See also, Stanley Lebergott, *Pursuing Happiness: American Consumers in the Twentieth Century* (Princeton: Princeton University Press, 1993).

5. David C. C. Mowery and Nathan Rosenberg, *Technology and the Pursuit of Economic Growth* (New York: Cambridge University Press, 2002), chapter 8.

6. Philip Seib, *Rush Hour* (Fort Worth: The Summit Group, 1994), p. 157.

7. Jane Brody, "America's Health: An Assessment," *New York Times Magazine*, Oct. 8th, 1989.

8. In general, Charles Seller's *The Market Revolution*. See Avner Offer for many related issues and, in particular, the regard economy, as

he calls it, *The Challenge of Affluence: Self-control and Well-being in the United States Since 1850* (New York: Oxford University Press, 2006).

9. Alexander Keyssar, *Out of Work: The First Century of Unemployment in Massachusetts* (New York: Cambridge University Press, 1986).

10. "Outsourcing of Manufacturing Employment," http://www.nikutai-to-kageboushi.com/outsourc.html (last visited Nov. 21, 2008.

11. See Robert Samuelson, who has persistently and strenuously claimed this. *The Good Life and Its Discontents: The American Dream in the Age of Entitlement* (New York: Random House, 1995).

12. Anthony Carnevale and Stephen Rose, *Education for What? The Office Economy* (Princeton: Educational Testing Service, 1998).

13. See the original paper, Paul David, "The Computer and the Dynamo: The Modern Productivity Paradox in a Not-Too-Distant Mirror," in *Technology and Productivity: The Challenge for Economic Policy* (OECD, 1991).

14. I have summarized some of this research and provided my own views in *The End of Affluence* (New York: Random House, 1995), and *Why Economies Grow* (New York: Basic Books/Century Foundation, 2002).

15. Richard R. Nelson and Gavin Wright, "The Rise and Fall of American Technological Leadership: The Postwar Era in Historical Perspective," *Journal of Economic Literature,* December, 1992, p. 1939.

16. Jared Bernstein, "Real Wages Decline in 2007," Economic Policy Institute, January 16, 2008 | EPI Issue Brief #240. http://www.epi.org/content.cfm/ib240

17. In general, the data cited here are conventional government statistics. The sources are the Bureau of Labor Statistics, the Bureau of Economic Analysis, and the U.S. Census Bureau, which compiles statistics such as the Consumer Population Survey for the BLS. I will not repeatedly cite sources for forthcoming statistics, unless they were dependent on analysis by individual economists that may be controversial.

18. Early writers on this theme include, Susan Faludi, *Stiffed: The Betrayal of the American Man* (New York: William Morrow, 1991); Frank Levy, *Dollars and Dreams: The Changing American Income Distribution* (New York: Russell Sage, 1987).

19. A striking summary of these issues can be found in Robert Haveman and Timothy Smeeding, "The Role of Education in Social Mobility," and "Opportunity in America," editors Isabell Sawhill and Sara McLanahan, issue of *The Future of Children* (Princeton and Washington D.C.: Woodrow Wilson School of Public Policy and International Affairs and Brookings Institution, 2006), pp. 125–49.

20. All data cited are gathered and published by the Bureau of Economic Analysis of the Commerce Department, Bureau of Labor Statistics of the Labor Department, or the Bureau of the Census.

21. Jeff Madrick and Nikolaos Papanikolaou, *The Stagnation of Males Wages* (New York: Schwartz Center for Economic Policy Analysis, 2008) (http://www.newschool.edu/cepa/).

22. Angus Maddison, *Dynamic Forces in Capitalist Development: A Long-Run Comparative View* (New York: Oxford University Press, 1991).

23. Isabel Sawhill and John E. Morton, "Economic Mobility: Is the American Dream Alive and Well?" in *Economic Mobility Project: The Pew Charitable Trusts* (Washington, DC: Brookings Institution Press, 2007). http://www.brookings.edu/~/media/Files/rc/papers/2007/05us economics_morton/05useconomics_morton.pdf. Frank Levy and Peter Temlin, "Inequality and Institutions on 20th Century America," Industrial Performance Center Working Paper Series (Boston: Department of Economics, Massachusetts Institute of Technology, 2007).

24. Lee Rainwater and Timothy Smeeding, *Poor Kids in a Rich Country: America's Children in Comparative Perspective* (New York: Russell Sage Foundation, 2003).

25. Among other sources, Marque-Luisa Miringoff and Sandra Opdycke, *America's Social Health, Putting Social Issues Back on the Agenda* (New York: M.E. Sharpe, 2008). On child poverty, in particular, see Smeeding and Rainwater, *Poor Kids in a Rich Country*; The Justice Policy Institute, "Cellblocks or Classrooms? The Funding of Higher Education and Corrections and Its Impact on African American Men," 2002 (www.justicepolicy.org).

26. Sawhill and John, "Economic Mobility: Is the American Dream Alive and Well?"

27. Thomas Piketty and Emmanuel Saez, "Income Inequality in the

United States, 1913–1998." *The Quarterly Journal of Economics.* Vol. CXVIII, Issue 1, 2003, pp. 1–39.

28. Richard G. Wilkinson offers a provocative if contentious overview regarding health and inequality, *The Impact of Inequality: How To Make Sick Societies Healthier* (New York: The New Press, 2005). See also Avner Offer, *The Challenge of Affluence* for an excellent and balanced overview of issues concerning affluence and happiness.

29. Samuelson, *The Good Life.*

30. Gordon S. Wood, *Radicalism of the American Revolution*, (New York: Knopf, 1993), p. 123.

31. See Kevin M. Murphy and Robert H. Topel for the classic if controversial paper, "The Value of Life, the Economic Benefits of Longevity" (Chicago: Stigler Center for the Study of the Economy and the State, University of Chicago, 2006), http://www.chicagogsb.edu/capideas/feb06/1.aspx (last visited March 11, 2007).

32. The Bureau of Labor Statistics offsets automobile inflation for improvements in quality, such as durability. But for the most part, American consumers pay for the improved quality.

33. The report by the Boskin Commission in 1997 is the leading paper on this subject. There have been many rebuttals. See Jeff Madrick, "The Cost of Living: A New Myth," *New York Review of Books*, March 6, 1997. More recently, see an excellent set of essays in "The Symposium on the Boskin Commission Report A Decade Later," *International Productivity Monitor*, Number 12, Spring 2006, Ottawa; particularly two pieces by economist Jack Triplet.

34. Elizabeth Warren and Amelia Warren Tyagi, *The Two-Income Trap: Why Middle-class Mothers and Fathers Are Going Broke* (New York: Basic Books, 2003).

35. See Madrick, *Why Economies Grow*, p. 223.

36. Robert Haveman and Timothy Smeeding, *The Role of Higher Education in Social Mobility,* The Future of Children, Vol. 16, No. 2, Opportunity in America (October 2006), pp. 125–50.

37. Jeff Madrick, William Milberg, and Melissa Mahoney, *State Market Relations for a Globalized Economy* (Schwartz Center for Economic Policy Analysis, Policy Notes, April 2006).

38. Mishel et al., *The State of Working America, 2006/2007*, pp. 148–51.

39. Madrick and Papanikoloaou, *The Stagnation of Male Wages*.

40. Mishel, et al., *The State of Working America 2006/2007*, p. 119.

41. A classic work on this issue is by two law professors, Lucian Bebchuk and Jesse Fried, *Pay Without Performance:The Unfulfillfed Promise of Executive Compensation* (Cambridge: Harvard University Press, 2004). Also, more current, Lucian Bebchuk andYaniv Grinstein, "The Growth of Executive Pay," *Oxford Review of Economic Policy*, Vol. 21, 2005, pp. 283–303.

42. Wilkinson, *The Impact of Inequality,* in particular, the first three chapters.

43. Mishel, et al., *The State of Working America*, p. 111.

44. Dean Baker, *The Productivity to Paycheck Gap: What the Data Show, The Real Cause of Lagging Wages* (Washington D.C.: Center for Economic and Policy Research [CEPR], 2007).

45. Ibid., p. 136.

46. Again, Haveman and Smeeding provide the best survey of the evidence, *The Role of Higher Education in Social Mobility*, pp. 125–50.

47. William Chase, *NewYork Times* Op-Ed, September 5th, 2006.

48. Jolene Kirschenman and Kathryn M. Neckerman, "We'd Love to Hire Them, But. . . . The Meaning of Race for Employers," in *The Urban Underclass,* eds., Paul E. Peterson and Christopher Jencks (Washington, D.C.: Brookings Institution, 1991). For an excellent general overview, in which this study is cited, see Amanda E. Lewis, Maria Krysnan, Sharon M. Collins, Korie Edwards, and Geoff Ward, "Institutional patterns and Transformations: Race and Ethnicity in Housing, Education, Labor Markets, Religion and Criminal Justice," in *The Changing Terrain of Race and Ethnicity,* eds., Maria Krysnan and Amanda E. Lewis (NewYork: Russell Sage Foundation, 2004), pp. 67–119.

49. Henry Farber, "What Do We Know About Job Loss in the United States?" Federal Reserve Bank of Chicago, *Economic Perspectives*, Second Quarter, 2005.

50. Warren and Tyagi, *Two-Income Trap*. Among the recent works, Jacob Hacker, *The Great Risk Shift* (NewYork: Oxford University Press),

2006; Robin Blackburn, *Age Shock: How Finance Is Failing Us* (London: Verso, 2006); Teresa Ghilarducci, *When I'm Sixty-Four: The Plot against Pensions and the Plan to Save Them* (Princeton: Princeton University Press, 2008).

51. James Heckman, "The Productivity Argument for Investing in Children," Committee for Economic Development, Invest in Kids Working Group, Working Paper No. 5., Washington D.C., 2004; Janet Currie, "Early Childhood Education Programs," *Journal of Economic Perspectives*, Spring, 2001, pp. 213–38.

52. Robert G. Lynch, "Exceptional Returns, Economic, Fiscal and Social Benefits of Investment in Early Childhood Development," Economic Policy Institute, Washington D.C., 2004.

53. Wilkinson, *The Impact of Inequality*, in particular, p. 80.

54. Kevin Phillips, *American Theocracy: The Peril and Politics of Radical Religion, Oil, and Borrowed Money in the 21st Century* (New York: Viking, 2006), pp. 117–21.

55. Dynan, Karen E. and Donald L. Kohn, "The Rise in U.S. Household Indebtedness: Causes and Consequences," FEDS Working Paper No. 2007–37 (August 8, 2007).

PART III
WHAT TO DO

1. Robert J. Samuelson, *The Good Life and Its Discontents: The American Dream in the Age of Entitlement* (New York: Knopf, 1997).

2. Steve Rose, *The Trouble with Class Interest Populism*, Progressive Policy Institute, April 25th, 2006.

3. "Solar Grand Plan," *Scientific American,* Jan. 2008, Vol. 298, Issue 1, pp. 64–73.

4. Alan Blinder, *Economic Policy and the Great Stagflation* (Burlington, MA: Academic Press, 1980).

5. George A. Akerlof, William T. Dickens, and George L. Perry, *The Macroeconomics of Low Inflation*, Brookings Paper on Economic Activity, 1996 (1), pp. 1–59.

6. Daniel Aaronson and Bhashkar Mazumder, "Intergenerational

Economic Mobility in the U.S., 1940 to 2000," Working paper 2005–12, Federal Reserve Bank of Chicago, June 2006.

7. Haveman and Smeeding, *The Role of Higher Education in Social Mobility*, pp. 125–50.

8. In general, Alexander Keyssar, Stephan Thernstrom, and Robert Fogel (eds.), *Out of Work: The First Century of Unemployment in Massachusetts* (New York: Cambridge University Press, 1986).

9. Mishel et al., *State of Working America*, p. 250.

10. Edward N. Wolff (ed.), *International Perspectives on Household Wealth* (Northhampton, MA: Edward Elgar Publishing, 2006).

11. Edward N. Wolff and Richard C. Leone, *Top Heavy: Increasing Inequality of Wealth in America and What Can Be Done about It* (New York: New Press, 2001).

12. Again, see Avner Offer's summary of these issues in *The Challenge of Affluence*, in particular, pp. 233–69.

13. Ibid.

14. Congressional Budget Office, Budget Options, chapter 3, pp. 255–59, February, 2007.

15. Ibid., Budget Options, p. 270.

16. Joel Friedman, The Decline of Corporate Income Tax Revenues, Center on Budget and Policy Priorities, October 24, 2003, www.cbpp.org/10–16–03tax.htm (last accessed May 19, 2008).

17. Ibid., Extrapolating from CBO estimates, p. 260.

18. Ibid, Revenue Options, p. 323.

19. Tom Redburn, "The Real Climate Debate: To Cap or To Tax," *The New York Times*, http://www.nytimes.com/2007/11/02/us/politics/04web-redburn.html?_r=1&oref=slogin (Accessed Nov. 3, 2007).

20. As noted earlier, Lindert argues that a high sales tax—valued added tax—in Europe has contributed substantially to growth by encouraging savings (*Growing Public*, p. 131).

21. Tax revenues based on analysis by Robert McIntyre, Citizens for Tax Justice, Washington D.C..

22. Infrastructure Management Group and Government Finance Group, *An Evaluation of the TE-045 Innovative Finance Research Initiative*, prepared for the U.S. Federal Highway Administration (FHWA), Octo-

ber 1996. The job estimate is from the FHWA itself, not the consultants, and is cited in the section on "Impacts of Increased Investment on Job Creation," http://www.fhwa.dot.gov/innovativefinance/evalch3.htm.

23. James Heckman and L. Lochner, "Rethinking Education and Training Policy: Understanding the Sources of Skill Formation in a Modern Economy," in *Securing the Future: Investing in Children From Birth to College*, eds. S. Danziger and J. Waldfogel (New York: Russell Sage Foundation, 2000).

24. See Robert Lynch, *Enriching Children, Enriching the Nation: Public Investment in High-Quality Prekindergarten* (Washington, D.C.: Economic Policy Institute, 2007).

25. William Dickens and Charles Buschnagel, "Dynamic Estimates of Fiscal Effects of Investing in Preschool Education" (Washington, D.C.: Brookings Institution, 2007).

26. For a pro-business summary, see Fishback, *Government and the American Economy*.

27. Leading works making these contentions, in order are: Benjamin M. Friedman and Michael C. Jensen, *Foundations of Organization Strategy* (Cambridge: Harvard University Press, 1983); Joel Mokyr, *The Lever of Riches, Technological Creativity and Economic Progress* (New York: Oxford University Press, 1990).

28. Mishel et al., *State of Working America 2006/2007*, p. 110. Robert J. Gordon and Ian Dew-Becker, "Unresolved Issues in the rise of Inequality in America," paper presented at the AEA meetings, Chicago, January, 2007 (http://faculty-web.at.northwestern.edu/economics/gordon/ChiAEA_RJG_Penner_RJGrevIDBcomments_070102.pdf (last visited Nov. 25, 2007).

29. Dale W. Jorgenson and Kevin J. Stiroh, 2000. "Raising the Speed Limit: U.S. Economic Growth in the Information Age," OECD Economics Department Working Paper 261, OECD, Brussels. Also, Gordon and Dew-Becker, ibid.

30. Lance Taylor, Scepa Working Paper Number, 2007.

31. Aaronson and Mazumder, "Intergenerational Economic Mobility . . . "

32. Mishel, et al., *State of Working America 2006/2007*, p. 190.

33. Robert Pollin, "What is a Living Wage? Considerations from Santa Monica, Ca.," pollin@econs.umass.edu (last visited Jan, 4, 2008).

34. Mishel, et al., *State of Working America 2006/2007*, p. 183.

35. Chirag Mehta and Nok Theodore, "Undermining the Right to Organize: Employer Behavior During Union Representation Campaigns (Chicago: University of Illinois at Chicago, 2005).

36. Lawrence D. Bobo, "Inequalities that Endure? Racial Ideology, American Politics, and the Peculiar Role of the Social Sciences," in *The Changing Terrain of Race and Ethnicity*, eds. Krysnan and Lewis, p. 33.

37. Kirschenman and Neckerman, "We'd Love to Hire Them."

38. William Bowen and Derek Bok, *The Shape of the River* (Princeton: Princeton University Press, 1998).

39. For the success of the Swedish system of wage cooperation, see Pontusson, "Whither Social Europe?"

40. Edward M. Kennedy, *American Back on Track* (New York: Viking, 2006), p. 98.

41. Lindert, *Growing Public,* pp. 254–57.

42. Marcia Meyers and Janet Gornick, *Work/Family Reconciliation Policies for the United States: Lesson from Abroad* (University of Washington & City University of New York, 2004).

43. Jeffrey Stoddard, Robert F. St. Peter, and Paul Newacheck, "Health insurance and ambulatory care for Children," *New England Journal of Medicine*, 330(20), 1421–25.

44. Peter S. Hussey, Gerard F. Anderson, Robin Osborn, Colin Feek, Vivienne McLaughlin, Jon Miller, and Arnold Epstein, "How Does the Quality of Care Compare in Five Countries?" *Health Affairs,* Vol. 23, Issue 3, 2004.

45. Kennedy, *American Back on Track*, pp. 132–33.

46. U.S. Department of Education, *Empty Promises: The Myth of College Access in America: A Report of the Advisory Committee on Student Financial Assistance,* Washington, D.C., June 2002. For a fine overview, again, Haveman and Smeeding, *The Role of Higher Education in Social Mobility*, pp. 125–50.

47. Mark Dudzic and Adolph Reed Jr., "Free for All: Free Tuition at All Public Colleges and Universities for Students Who Meet Admission Standards," *The Nation*, February 5, 2004.

48. American Society of Civil Engineers. 2005. *Report Card for America's Infrastructure*, available at www.asce.org/reportcard/2005/index .cfm (last visited Feb. 5, 2008).

49. See the website of the Energy Information Administration, United States Department of Energy (www.eia.doe.gov).

50. U.S. Department of Transportation (DOT), Federal Highway Administration, and Federal Transit Administration, *2006 Status of the Nation's Highways, Bridges, and Transit: Executive Summary*. Washington, 2006, p. vi. Available at: www.fhwa.dot.gov/policy/2006cpr/pdfs/ esblue.pdf (last visited Feb. 5, 2008).

51. See sources above and in general, Congressional Budget Office, *Trends in Public Spending on Transportation and Water Infrastructure, 1956 to 2004* (Washington, D.C.: August 2007). The data in the CBO report comes from the Office of Management and Budget (OMB) and the Census Bureau.

52. Ibid. Also, Francisco Rodriguz, 2006. "Have Collapses in Infrastructure Spending Led to Cross-Country Divergence in Per Capita GDP?" Working Paper no. 2006–013, *Wesleyan Economics* (April).

53. For more information, see www.apolloalliance.org

54. For full discussions of these issues, see Alicia H. Munnell and Steven A. Sass, *Working Longer: The Answer to the Retirement Income Challenge* (Washington, D.C.: Brookings Institution Press, 2008); Teresa Ghilarducci, *When I'm Sixty-Four: The Plot against Pensions and the Plan to Save Them* (Princeton: Princeton University Press, 2008); Robin Blackburn, *Age Shock, How Finance is Failing Us* (London: Verso, 2007).

55. National Employment Law Project, "Changing Workforce, Changing Economy, State Unemployment Insurance Reforms for the 21st Century," 2004.

56. Greg Mastel, "Why We Should Expand Trade Adjustment Assistance," *Challenge Magazine*, September/October, 2006.

57. Jeffrey H. Birnbaum, "The Road to Riches Is Called K Street,

Lobbying Firms Hire More, Pay More, Charge More to Influence Government," *Washington Post*, June 22, 2005, p. A01

58. Alan Brinkley, *End of Reform: New Deal Liberalism in Recession and War* (New York: Knopf, 1996), p. 257.

59. Jeff Madrick, *Breaking the Stranglehold on Growth,* The Economic Policy Institute, EPI Briefing Paper #192, June 22, 2007.

INDEX

■■■■■■■■■■■■■■

analysis of, 141–42; economic
benefits of, 59–60, 127–28; of
the financial industry (*see* financial
regulation); of land distribution
in early America, 33–35; in the
Progressive Era, 50–52; proposals for a pragmatic government
addressing change, 169–71.
See also deregulation
Republicans: antigovernment ideology, support for, 1–2; denial of
poor economic performance in
recent decades, reasons for,
100–1
research and development (R&D),
the federal government and,
57–58
Riis, Jacob, 49
Rockefeller, John D., 49
Roosevelt, Franklin D., 29, 55–56
Roosevelt, Theodore, 50
Rosenberg, Nathan, 183n.1

Samuelson, Robert, 125
savings, low rate of, 130–32
Sawhill, Isabel, 94
Scalia, Antonin, 28
Securities and Exchange Commission, 55
services economy, capitalist assumptions regarding the transition to,
72–74
sexual discrimination, 152
Sinclair, Upton, 49
single-parent families, 154–55
Slemrod, Joel, 15
Smith, Adam, 25, 32–33, 35,
38–39, 45, 59

social Darwinism, 48
Social Security: Eisenhower's expansion of, 57; enactment of, 54–55;
proposals regarding, 165–67; as
violation of rights, conservative
view of, 28
social spending/transfers: Clinton's
reduction of, 3–5; feasibility of
expanding, 128–29; Friedman's
argument against, 23–24 (*see also*
Friedman, Milton); government
resistance to in the late nineteenth century, 48; increases in
between 1948 and 1970, 58;
level of and economic growth,
14–20; New Deal increases in,
55–56; in the Progressive Era,
50–51; proposals for a pragmatic
government addressing change,
144–46, 154–65
Society of Civil Engineers, 139
Solow, Robert, 183n.1
Spencer, Herbert, 48
standard of living: constant gains
in, loss of, 94; damage to in recent
decades, 10, 83–87; denial of stagnating, reasons for, 99–102; the
education (and class) divide and,
85–87; family income in recent
decades and the declining, 92–94;
the gender divide and, 84–85;
growth in productivity and, gap
between in the early 2000s, 111;
new sources of anxiety as factors
in assessing, 113–15; real wages
in recent decades and the declining, 87–92; rising costs and, difficulty of accounting for, 104–6;